Then Sings My Soul

Edited by William D. Killen

"Give thanks to the Lord, call on His name." –Psalm 105:1

Kravitz & Sons

INNOVATORS IN PUBLISHING, MARKETING AND ADVERTISING

Kravitz and Sons LLC
204 E Arlington Blvd. Suite B
Greenville, NC 27858

Published by Kravitz and Sons LLC.

ISBN: 979-8-89639-555-3 (sc)
ISBN: 979-8-89639-556-0 (e)

Acknowledgments

Many of these short stories are individual works of art and include works that are fiction and where possible have been identified as fiction. I included some of these fiction works because of the message and also the humor.

I want to thank Jim Atkinson, John Buckman, Jim Golden, Ken Henry, Jennifer Keaney, Justin Keaney, Mark Killen, Jack McElfish, Mike Merwick, Betty Murphy, Lynn Parker, Bill Roberts, Ronald Scott, Tyler Scott, Charles Shupienus, John Stapleton, Gary Taylor and Brenda Vaccarelli for the many emails they shared over the years as well as individual works of art.

A special thanks to Mark and Penny Derrick, Ken Henry, and Ronald and Tyler Scott for their review and critique of this book. Where possible the source of the material is identified such as "*Distributed by email - Author unknown*" or "*Distributed by email – Author identified*" or "*Downloaded from the Internet.*"

A SPECIAL THANKS to Liz Brockman for the outstanding work on designing the covers for this book. This is the fifth book cover Liz has designed for me.

There are several items contained within that were written by family members and a lot of "stuff" I wrote in high school, including a 12th grade English Class assignment, "The Locker Room."

A special thanks to my friend Kelvin Cochran for appearing on the cover and his contributions to this book. Kelvin, a born-again Christian, was a successful fire chief in Louisiana and Georgia, dedicated to promoting a workplace culture without racism, sexism, cronyism, or favoritism.

Kelvin was fired in January, 2015 for "discrimination." Kelvin authored "*Who Told You That You Were Naked?*" a 162-page men's Bible study book, wherein he explained biblical marriage and sexuality. The Atlanta Mayor reacting to "political correctness run amok" suspended Kelvin without pay after some of his employees complained about the content of his self-published religious book. Among other things, the book calls "homosexuality" and "lesbianism" a "sexual perversion" morally equivalent to "pederasty" and "bestiality."

The book, written at home, is intended to guide men on how to live a faith-filled, virtuous life. It says "sex outside the confines of marriage between a man and a woman" — such as sodomy, homosexuality, lesbianism, adultery, fornication and lasciviousness — are contrary to God's will, according to the Bible.

"Give thanks to the Lord, call on His name." –Psalm 105:1

Dedication

This book is dedicated to Carole Jean Hursey, the love of my life, my confidant, my friend, the mother of our four beautiful children and the one who has kept me on track for the past 67 plus years. Thank you Lord for such a wonderful partner and best friend.

"Give thanks to the Lord, call on His name." –Psalm 105:1

Foreword

A few years ago, on a flight to Los Angeles I was reminiscing about the International Association of Fire Chiefs Study Mission to Israel and the visits we made to the Holy Land. Then there were thoughts about all of the emails received over the years with the caveat "If you love Jesus pass it on."

Some I passed on, most I copied to a file labeled "Wisdom, Trivia and other interesting information." I was thinking one day I might compile the information and publish it in a book. Some of the material was spiritual, encouraging, motivational, and funny.

Well that "one day" is here and the purpose of this book is to glorify God and share some of the Christian humor I accumulated from emails and friends. There are several heartwarming motivational stories in this book and lots of humor, whether it is a church bulletin blooper, something a child said, or something someone created to generate a laugh.

Many of the stories herein are humorous and are included to provide the impetus to cause the reader to laugh, several stories serve to encourage or motivate and many are solely intended to glorify God and His love for His children.

Through these pages I hope the reader will see God's love and that God has a sense of humor. The title chosen for this book is from a stanza in "How Great Thou Art", one of my favorite hymns; which was written in 1885 and popularized by George Beverly Shea and Cliff Barrows during the Billy Graham evangelistic crusades between 1947 and 2005. I have fond memories from the National Capitol Crusade in Washington, DC during the summer of 1960.

I believe God has a great sense of humor and wants us to laugh. Just look at some of His creations, many of them will make you laugh. Several verses of scripture speak of laughter.

Scriptures quoted herein are from the New International Version of the Holy Bible.

- *"God has brought me laughter, and everyone who hears about this will laugh with me."* **Genesis 21:6**

- *Then our mouth was filled with <u>laughter</u> then, and our tongues with shouts of joy; then they said among the nations, "The Lord has done great things for them."* **Psalm 126:2**

"Give thanks to the Lord, call on His name." –Psalm 105:1

- *A time to weep, and a time to <u>laugh</u>; a time to mourn, and a time to dance;* **Ecclesiastes 3:4**

- *"Blessed are you who are hungry now, for you shall be satisfied. "Blessed are you who weep now, for you shall <u>laugh</u>.* **Luke 6:21**

- *"He will yet fill your mouth with <u>laughter</u> and your lips with shouting.* **Job 8:21**

- *"A cheerful heart is a good medicine."* **Proverbs 17:22**

A joyful noise unto the Lord could be laughter, especially a baby's laughter and the laughter of little children.

It doesn't matter how many people you share this book with, just remember if it made you laugh, your friends will laugh too.

Enjoy the laughter! - We all need it ---

"Give thanks to the Lord, call on His name." –Psalm 105:1

Table of Contents

"Give thanks to the Lord, call on His name." –Psalm 105:1

Something to ponder…

Never thought of it…

Never thought of it! **Jesus** died over 2000 years ago. Nobody has ever referred to **HIM** as the late **Jesus**, Not even the heathens. Nowhere in history. Nowhere has **HE** ever been referred to in the past tense **HE 'is'** the **Living God**! When **Jesus** died on the cross **HE** was thinking of you!

Email from Bill Roberts
June 30, 2017

Who told you that you were naked?

A Profound Question. "Who told you that you were naked? meant much more than, "Who told you that you do not have on clothes?" From God's perspective nakedness meant so much more. It meant condemnation and deprivation to his most precious creation-mankind. Though He reconciled Adam's condition by clothing him in coats of lambs' skin, Adam never got over what he had done. Condemnation has dominated ever since. Now we have a more permanent solution. We have been clothed with Christ! Redeemed men who carry the curse of condemnation and deprivation cannot fulfill their purpose as husbands, fathers, community and business leaders-world changers! Adam never gave God a straight answer. It is time to answer the question, WHO TOLD YOU THAT YOU WERE NAKED?

By Kelvin J. Cochran
November, 2015

"Give thanks to the Lord, call on His name." –Psalm 105:1

I Asked God

Distributed by email - Author unknown

I asked God for water, He gave me an ocean.

I asked God for a flower, He gave me a garden.

I asked God for a friend, He gave me all of YOU.

If God brings you to it, He will bring you through it.

Awesome!!

We complain about the cross we bear but don't realize it is preparing us for the dip in the road that God can see and we cannot.

Whatever your cross, whatever your pain,
      there will always be sunshine, after the rain....

Perhaps you may stumble, perhaps even fall;
      But God's always ready, to answer your call....

He knows every heartache, sees every tear,
      a word from His lips, can calm every fear...

Your sorrows may linger, throughout the night,
      But suddenly vanish, by dawn's early light...

The Savior is waiting, somewhere above,
      to give you His grace, and send you His love.

May God fill your day with blessings!! Be kinder than necessary, for everyone you meet is fighting some kind of battle!

Email from Charles Shupienus
June 22, 2017

"Let your light shine before others, so that they may see your good works and give glory to your Father who is in heaven."

"Give thanks to the Lord, call on His name." —Psalm 105:1

Ten Commandments to Follow in Life

Someone has written these beautiful words. Must read and try to understand the deep meaning of it. They are like the ten commandments to follow in life all the time.

1. Prayer is not a "spare wheel" that you pull out when in trouble, but it is a "steering wheel" that directs the right path throughout.

2. So why is a car's windshield so large and the rear-view mirror so small? Because our past is not as important as our future. So, look ahead and move on.

3. Friendship is like a book. It takes a few seconds to burn, but it takes years to write.

4. All things in life are temporary. If it's going well, enjoy it, that won't last long. If it's going badly, don't worry, that won't last long either.

5. Old friends are gold! New friends are diamond! If you get a diamond, don't forget the gold! Because to hold a diamond, you always need a base of gold!

6. Often when we lose hope and think this is the end, God smiles from above and says, "Relax, sweetheart, it's just a bend, not the end!"

7. When God solves your problems, you have faith in His abilities; When God doesn't solve your problems, He has faith in your abilities.

8. A blind person asked St. Anthony, "Can there be anything worse than losing eye sight?"

He replied, "Yes, losing your vision!"

9. When you pray for others, God listens to you and blesses them; Sometimes, when you are safe and happy, remember that someone has prayed for you.

10. Worrying does not take away tomorrow's troubles, it takes away today's peace.

Email from John Stapleton
May 27, 2017

"Give thanks to the Lord, call on His name." –Psalm 105:1

God's Accuracy

One may observe God's accuracy in the hatching of eggs. . .. those of the canary in 14 days; those of the barnyard hen in 21 days; eggs of ducks and geese in 28 days; those of the mallard in 35 days; the eggs of the parrot and the ostrich hatch in 42 days. (NOTICE, THEY ARE ALL DIVISIBLE BY SEVEN, THE NUMBER OF DAYS IN A WEEK!)

See God's wisdom in the making of an ELEPHANT. . . The four legs of this great beast all bend forward in the same direction. No other quadruped is so made. God planned that this animal would have a huge body- too large to live on two legs. For this reason, He gave it four fulcrums so that it can rise from the ground easily.

The HORSE rises from the ground on its two front legs first. A COW rises from the ground with its two hind legs first.

HOW WISE THE LORD IS IN ALL HIS WORKS OF CREATION!

Each Watermelon has an even number of stripes on the rind. Each Orange has an even number of segments. Each Ear of Corn has an even number of rows. Each Stalk of Wheat has an even number of grains. Every Bunch of Bananas has on its lowest row an even number of bananas, and each row decreases by one, so that one row has an even number and the next row an odd number.

AMAZING! THERE'S MORE...

The waves of the sea roll in on shore twenty-six to the minute in all kinds of weather. All grains are found in even numbers on the stalks. God has caused the flowers to blossom at certain specified times during the day. Linnaeus, the great botanist, once said that if he had a conservatory containing the right kind of soil, moisture, and temperature, he could tell the time of day or night by the flowers that were open and those that were closed.

The lives of each of us may be ordered by the Lord in a beautiful way for His glory, if we will only entrust Him with our lives. If we try to regulate our own lives, we will have only mess and failure.

Only God, who made our brains and hearts, can successfully guide them to a profitable end.

Email from Charles Shupienus 2017

"Give thanks to the Lord, call on His name." –Psalm 105:1

Love

Love is friendship that has caught fire. It is quiet understanding, mutual confidence, sharing and forgiving. It is loyalty through good and bad times. It settles for less than perfection and makes allowances for human weaknesses.

Love is content with the present, it hopes for the future, and it doesn't brood over the past. It's the day-in and day-out chronicle of irritations, problems, compromises small disappointments, big victories and working toward common goals.

If you have love in your life, it can make up for a great many things you lack. If you don't have it, no matter what else there is, it's not enough.

By Ann Landers circulated via internet

Noah's Ark

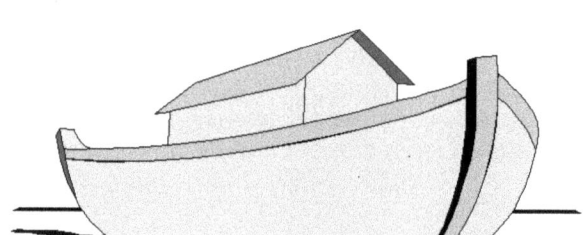

Everything I need to know, I learned from Noah's Ark.

ONE: Don't miss the boat.

TWO: Remember that we are all in the same boat!

THREE: Plan ahead. It wasn't raining when Noah built the Ark.

FOUR: Stay fit. When you're 80 years old, someone may ask you to do something really big.

FIVE: Don't listen to critics; just get on with the job that needs to be done.

SIX: Build your future on high ground.

SEVEN: For safety's sake, travel in pairs.

"Give thanks to the Lord, call on His name." –Psalm 105:1

EIGHT: Speed isn't always an advantage. The snails were on board with the cheetahs.

NINE: When you're stressed, float awhile.

TEN: Remember, the Ark was built by amateurs; the Titanic by professionals.

ELEVEN: No matter the storm, there's always a rainbow waiting.

Email from John Stapleton
August 5, 2017

Editor's Note:

"*All I need to know I learned from Noah's Ark*" shared via email is found on numerous websites.

Moments
Distributed by email - Author unknown

Happy moments, praise God.
Difficult moments, seek God.
Quiet moments, worship God
Painful moments, trust God.
Every moment, thank God.

Isn't it strange?

1. Isn't it strange how a 20-dollar bill seems like such a large amount when you donate it to church, but such a small amount when you go shopping?

2. Isn't it strange how 2 hours seem so long when you're at church, and how short they seem when you're watching a good movie?

3. Isn't it strange that you can't find a word to say when you're praying, but you have no trouble thinking what to talk about with a friend?

4. Isn't it strange how difficult and boring it is to read one chapter of the Bible, but how easy it is to read 100 pages of a popular novel or ZANE GREY book?

5. Isn't it strange how everyone wants front-row-tickets to concerts or games, but they do whatever is possible to sit at the last row in Church?

"*Give thanks to the Lord, call on His name.*" –Psalm 105:1

6. Isn't it strange how we need to know about an event for Church 2-3 weeks before the day so we can include it in our agenda, but we can adjust it for other events at the last minute?

7. Isn't it strange how difficult it is to learn a fact about God to share it with others, but how easy it is to learn, understand, extend and repeat gossip?

8. Isn't it strange how we believe everything that magazines and newspapers say, but we question the words in the Bible?

9. Isn't it strange how everyone wants a place in heaven, but they don't want to believe, do, or say anything to get there?

10. Isn't it strange how we send jokes in e-mails and they are forwarded right away, but when we are going to send messages about God, we think about it twice before we share it with others?

.... IT'S STRANGE ISN'T IT?

God vs Science

This one will keep your attention to the end.......It really makes you think........

A science professor begins his school year with a lecture to the students, "Let me explain the problem science has with religion." The atheist professor of philosophy pauses before his class and then asks one of his new students to stand.

"You're a Christian, aren't you, son?" "Yes sir," the student says.

"So you believe in God?" "Absolutely."

"Is God good?" "Sure! God is good."

"Is God All-powerful? Can God do anything?" "Yes."

"Are you good or evil?" "The Bible says I'm evil."

The professor grins knowingly. "Aha! The Bible!" He considers for a moment. "Here's one for you. Let's say there's a sick person over here and you can cure him. You can do it. Would you help him; would you try?" "Yes sir, I would."

"So you're good...!"

"Give thanks to the Lord, call on His name." –Psalm 105:1

"I wouldn't say that."

"But why not say that, you'd help a sick and maimed person if you could. Most of us would if we could. But God doesn't."

The student does not answer, so the professor continues. "He doesn't, does he? My brother was a Christian who died of cancer, even though he prayed to Jesus to heal him. How is this Jesus good? Can you answer that one?"

The student remains silent.

"No, you can't, can you" the professor says. He takes a sip of water from a glass on his desk to give the student time to relax.

"Let's start again, young fella. Is God good?" "Er...yes," the student says.

"Is Satan good?" The student doesn't hesitate on this one. "No."

"Then where does Satan come from?" The student falters. "From God"

"That's right. God made Satan, didn't he? Tell me, son. Is there evil in this world? " "Yes, sir."

"Evil's everywhere, isn't it and God did make everything, correct?" "Yes."

"So who created evil?" The professor continued, "If God created everything, then God created evil, since evil exists, and according to the principle that our works define who we are, then God is evil."

Again, the student has no answer. "Is there sickness immorality, hatred, ugliness, all these terrible things, do they exist in this world?"

The student squirms on his feet. "Yes."

"So who created them?" The student does not answer again, so the professor repeats his question.

"Who created them?" There is still no answer. Suddenly the lecturer breaks away to pace in front of the classroom. The class is mesmerized. "Tell me," he continues onto another student. "Do you believe in Jesus Christ, son?"

The student's voice betrays him and cracks. "Yes, professor, I do."

The old man stops pacing. "Science says you have five senses you use to identify and observe the world around you. Have you ever seen Jesus?"

"Give thanks to the Lord, call on His name." –Psalm 105:1

"No sir. I've never seen Him."

"Then tell us if you've ever heard your Jesus?" "No, sir, I have not."

"Have you ever felt your Jesus? Tasted your Jesus or smelled your Jesus? Have you ever had any sensory perception of Jesus Christ, or God for that matter?"

"No, sir, I'm afraid I haven't."

"Yet you still believe in him?" "Yes."

"According to the rules of empirical, testable, demonstrable protocol, science says your God doesn't exist. What do you say to that, son?"

"Nothing," the student replies. "I only have my faith."

"Yes, faith," the professor repeats. "And that is the problem science has with God. There is no evidence, only faith."

The student stands quietly for a moment, before asking a question of His own. "Professor, is there such thing as heat?" "Yes," the professor replies. "There's heat."

"And is there such a thing as cold?" "Yes, son, there's cold too."

"No sir, there isn't."

The professor turns to face the student, obviously interested. The room suddenly becomes very quiet. The student begins to explain. "You can have lots of heat, even more heat, super-heat, mega-heat, unlimited heat, white heat, a little heat or no heat, but we don't have anything called 'cold'. We can hit up to 458 degrees below zero, which is no heat, but we can't go any further after that. There is no such thing as cold; otherwise we would be able to go colder than the lowest -458 degrees."

"Every body or object is susceptible to study when it has or transmits energy, and heat is what makes a body or matter have or transmit energy. Absolute zero (-458 F) is the total absence of heat. You see, sir, cold is only a word we use to describe the absence of heat. We cannot measure cold. Heat we can measure in thermal units because heat is energy. Cold is not the opposite of heat, sir, just the absence of it."

Silence across the room. A pen drops somewhere in the classroom, sounding like a hammer.

"Give thanks to the Lord, call on His name." –Psalm 105:1

"What about darkness, professor. Is there such a thing as darkness?"
"Yes," the professor replies without hesitation. "What is night if it isn't darkness?"

"You're wrong again, sir. Darkness is not something; it is the absence of something. You can have low light, normal light, bright light, flashing light, but if you have no light constantly you have nothing and it's called darkness, isn't it?"

That's the meaning we use to define the word." "In reality, darkness isn't. If it were, you would be able to make darkness darker, wouldn't you?"

The professor begins to smile at the student in front of him. This will be a good semester. "So what point are you making, young man?"

"Yes, professor. My point is, your philosophical premise is flawed to start with, and so your conclusion must also be flawed."

The professor's face cannot hide his surprise this time. "Flawed? Can you explain how?"

"You are working on the premise of duality," the student explains. "You argue that there is life and then there's death; a good God and a bad God. You are viewing the concept of God as something finite, something we can measure. Sir, science can't even explain a thought."

"It uses electricity and magnetism, but has never seen, much less fully understood either one. To view death as the opposite of life is to be ignorant of the fact that death cannot exist as a substantive thing.

Death is not the opposite of life, just the absence of it."

"Now tell me, professor. Do you teach your students that they evolved from monkeys?"

"If you are referring to the natural evolutionary process, young man, yes, of course I do."

"Have you ever observed evolution with your own eyes, sir?"
The professor begins to shake his head, still smiling, as he realizes where the argument is going. A very good semester, indeed.

"Since no one has ever observed the process of evolution at work and cannot even prove that this process is an on-going endeavor, are you not teaching your opinion, sir? Are you now not a scientist, but a preacher?"

"Give thanks to the Lord, call on His name." –Psalm 105:1

The class is in an uproar. The student remains silent until the commotion has subsided.

"To continue the point you were making earlier to the other student, let me give you an example of what I mean."

The student looks around the room. "Is there anyone in the class who has ever seen the professor's brain?" The class breaks out into laughter.

"Is there anyone here who has ever heard the professor's brain, felt the professor's brain, touched or smelt the professor's brain?

No one appears to have done so. So, according to the established rules of empirical, stable, demonstrable protocol, science says that you have no brain, with all due respect, sir."

"So if science says you have no brain, how can we trust your lectures, sir?"

Now the room is silent. The professor just stares at the student, his face unreadable.

Finally, after what seems an eternity, the old man answers. "I guess you'll have to take them on faith."

"Now, you accept that there is faith, and, in fact, faith exists with life," the student continues. "Now, sir, is there such a thing as evil?"

Now uncertain, the professor responds, "Of course, there is. We see it everyday. It is in the daily example of man's inhumanity to man. It is in the multitude of crimes and violence everywhere in the world. These manifestations are nothing else but evil."

To this the student replied, "Evil does not exist sir, or at least it does not exist unto itself.

Evil is simply the absence of God. It is just like darkness and cold, a word that man has created to describe the absence of God.

God did not create evil. Evil is the result of what happens when man does not have God's love present in his heart. It's like the cold that comes when there is no heat or the darkness that comes when there is no light."

The professor sat down.

"Give thanks to the Lord, call on His name." –Psalm 105:1

I've learned....

I've learned....
That the best classroom in the world is at the feet of an elderly person.

I've learned....
That when you're in love, it shows.

I've learned .....
That just one person saying to me, 'You've made my day!' makes my day.

I've learned....
That having a child fall asleep in your arms is one of the most peaceful feelings in the world.

I've learned.....
That being kind is more important than being right.

I've learned....
That you should never say no to a gift from a child.

I've learned....
That I can always pray for someone when I don't have the strength to help him in any other way.

I've learned....
That no matter how serious your life requires you to be, everyone needs a friend to act goofy with.

I've learned....
That sometimes all a person needs is a hand to hold and a heart to understand.

I've learned....
That simple walks with my father around the block on summer nights when I was a child did wonders for me as an adult.

I've learned....
That money doesn't buy class.

I've learned....
That it's those small daily happenings that make life so spectacular.

I've learned...
That under everyone's hard shell is someone who wants to be appreciated and loved.

"Give thanks to the Lord, call on His name." –Psalm 105:1

I've learned.....
That to ignore the facts does not change the facts.

I've learned...
That love, not time, heals all wounds.

I've learned....
That the easiest way for me to grow as a person is to surround myself with people smarter than I am.

I've learned....
That everyone you meet deserves to be greeted with a smile.

I've learned....
That no one is perfect until you fall in love with them.

I've learned...
That life is tough, but I'm tougher.

I've learned...
That opportunities are never lost; someone will take the ones you miss.

I've learned....
That I wish I could have told my Mom that I love her one more time before she passed away.

I've learned....
That one should keep his words both soft and tender, because tomorrow he may have to eat them.

I've learned...
That a smile is an inexpensive way to improve your looks.

I've learned.....
That when your newly born grandchild holds your little finger in his little fist, you're hooked for life.

I've learned....
That everyone wants to live on top of the mountain, but all the happiness and growth occurs while you're climbing it.

I've learned....
That the less time I have to work with, the more things I get done.

Written by Andrew Aitken "Andy" Rooney
1919 – 2011
Email from John Stapleton

"Give thanks to the Lord, call on His name." –Psalm 105:1

Today I wish you...

Today I wish you a day of ordinary miracles ~

 A fresh pot of coffee you didn't make yourself.
 An unexpected phone call from an old friend,
 Green stoplights on your way to work.
 The fastest line at the grocery store.
 A good sing-along song on the radio.
 Your keys found right where you left them.

God's Wings

A little something to put things in perspective.

An article in National Geographic several years ago provided an interesting picture of God's wings After a forest fire in Yellowstone National Park, forest rangers began their trek up a mountain to assess the inferno's damage.

One ranger found a bird literally petrified in ashes, perched statuesque on the ground at the base of a tree. Somewhat sickened by the eerie sight, he knocked over the bird with a stick. When he gently struck it, three tiny chicks scurried from under their dead mother's wings.

The loving mother, keenly aware of impending disaster, had carried her offspring to the base of the tree and had gathered them under her wings, instinctively knowing that the toxic smoke would rise.

She could have flown to safety but had refused to abandon her babies. When the blaze had arrived and the heat had scorched her small body, the mother had remained steadfast. Because she had been willing to die, so those under the cover of her wings would live.

"*He will cover you with his feathers, and under his wings you will find refuge.*"
Psalm 91:4

Being loved this much should make a difference in your life. Remember the One who loves you, and then be different because of it. Time waits for no one. Treasure every moment you have. You will treasure it even more when you can share it with someone special. To realize the value of a friend...lose one.

"Give thanks to the Lord, call on His name." –Psalm 105:1

Shoes in church
Distributed by email - Author unknown

I showered and shaved............. I adjusted my tie.
I got there and sat.............. In a pew, just in time.
Bowing my head in prayer......... As I closed my eyes.
I saw the shoe of the man next to me.... Touching my own. I sighed.
With plenty of room on either side...... I thought, "Why must our soles touch"
It bothered me, his shoe touching mine... But it didn't bother him much.
A prayer began: "Our Father"............. I thought, "This man with the shoes... has no pride.
They're dusty, worn, and scratched. Even worse, there are holes on the side!"
"Thank You for blessings," the prayer went on. The shoe man said.............. a quiet "Amen."
I tried to focus on the prayer....... But my thoughts were on his shoes again.
Aren't we supposed to look our best... When walking through that door
"Well, this certainly isn't it," I thought, Glancing toward the floor.
Then the prayer was ended............ And the songs of praise began.
The shoe man was certainly loud...... Sounding proud as he sang.
His voice lifted the rafters......... His hands were raised high.
The Lord could surely hear... The shoe man's voice from the sky.
It was time for the offering....... And what I threw in was steep.
I watched as the shoe man reached.... Into his pockets so deep.
I saw what was pulled out.......... What the shoe man put in.
Then I heard a soft "clink" as when silver hits tin.
The sermon really bored me.......... To tears, and that's no lie.
It was the same for the shoe man... For tears fell from his eyes.
At the end of the service...... As is the custom here.
We must greet new visitors... And show them all good cheer.
But I felt moved somehow............. And wanted to meet the shoe man.
So, after the closing prayer........ I reached over and shook his hand.
He was old and his skin was dark.... And his hair was truly a mess.
But I thanked him for coming......... For being our guest.
He said, "My names' Charlie.......... I'm glad to meet you, my friend."
There were tears in his eyes....... But he had a large, wide grin.
"Let me explain," he said......... Wiping tears from his eyes.
"I've been coming here for months.... And you're the first to say 'Hi.'"
"I know that my appearance........."Is not like all the rest.
"But I really do try................"To always look my best."
"I always clean and polish my shoes..."Before my very long walk.
"But by the time I get here........."They're dirty and dusty, like chalk."
My heart filled with pain............ and I swallowed to hide my tears.
As he continued to apologize......... For daring to sit so near.
He said, "When I get here..........."I know I must look a sight.

"Give thanks to the Lord, call on His name." –Psalm 105:1

"But I thought if I could touch you..."Then maybe our souls might unite."
I was silent for a moment............ Knowing whatever was said
Would pale in comparison... I spoke from my heart, not my head.
"Oh, you've touched me," I said......"And taught me, in part;
"That the best of any man............"Is what is found in his heart."
The rest, I thought, ... This shoe man will never know.
Like just how thankful I really am... That his dirty old shoe touched my soul

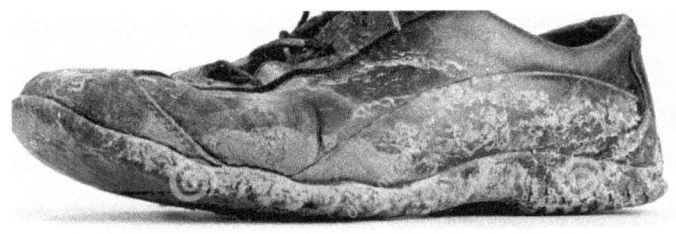

"What, then, shall we say in response to this? If God is for us, who can be against us?" **Romans 8:31**

Keep these thoughts with you throughout the coming years!

1. If God had a refrigerator, your picture would be on it.

2. If He had a wallet, your photo would be in it.

3. He sends you flowers every spring and a sunrise every morning.

4. Whenever you want to talk, He'll listen

5. He could live anywhere in the universe, and He chose your heart.

6. What about the Christmas gift He sent you in Bethlehem; not to mention that Friday at Calvary.

"Give thanks to the Lord, call on His name." *–Psalm 105:1*

Christian Ways to Reduce Stress.....

An Angel says, 'Never borrow from the future. If you worry about what may happen tomorrow and it doesn't happen, you have worried in vain. Even if it does happen, you have to worry twice.'

1. Pray.

2. Go to bed on time.

3. Get up on time so you can start the day unrushed.

4. Say no to projects that won't fit into your time schedule, or that will compromise your mental health.

5. Delegate tasks to capable others.

6. Simplify and unclutter your life.

7. Less is more. (Although one is often not enough, two are often too many.)

8. Allow extra time to do things and to get to places.

9. Pace yourself. Spread out big changes and difficult projects over time; don't lump the hard things all together.

10. Take one day at a time.

11. Separate worries from concerns. If a situation is a concern, find out what God would have you do and let go of the anxiety. If you can't do anything about a situation, forget it.

12. Live within your budget; don't use credit cards for ordinary purchases.

13. Have backups; an extra car key in your wallet, an extra house key buried in the garden, extra stamps, etc.

14. K.Y.M.S. (Keep Your Mouth Shut). This single piece of advice can prevent an enormous amount of trouble.

15. Do something for the Kid in You every day.

16. Carry a Bible with you to read while waiting in line.

17. Get enough rest.

"Give thanks to the Lord, call on His name." –Psalm 105:1

18. Eat right.

19 Get organized so everything has its place.

20. Listen to a tape while driving that can help improve your quality of life.

21. Write down thoughts and inspirations.

22. Every day, find time to be alone.

23. Having problems? Talk to God on the spot. Try to nip small problems in the bud. Don't wait until it's time to go to bed to try and pray

24. Make friends with Godly people.

25. Keep a folder of favorite scriptures on hand.

26. Remember that the shortest bridge between despair and hope is often a good 'Thank you Jesus.'

27. Laugh.

28. Laugh some more!

29. Take your work seriously, but not yourself at all.

30. Develop a forgiving attitude (most people are doing the best they can).

31. Be kind to unkind people (they probably need it the most).

32. Sit on your ego.

33 Talk less; listen more.

34. Slow down.

35. Remind yourself that you are not the general manager of the universe.

36. Every night before bed, think of one thing you're grateful for that you've never been grateful for before.

GOD HAS A WAY OF TURNING THINGS AROUND FOR YOU.

"Give thanks to the Lord, call on His name." –Psalm 105:1

Prayers and Inspirational Poems...

When Dinner Bells Ring

"When dinner bells ring and we all fly to eat at the bountiful table of love,
Why there's a suggestion that I want to make to the Master who rules above,
Give my honey and milk to somebody else, and put down on my plate, if you please,
Cornbread and onions and piled alongside, a big helping of plain black-eyed peas."

Samuel M. Smith
1922-1992

A.S.A.P.

Always Say a Prayer

"God, our Father, if it is Your will, walk through my house and the houses of my friends, take away all my worries and illnesses and those of my friends, please watch over and heal my family and the families of my friends, in Jesus name, Amen.'

Email from Bill Roberts
June 30, 2017

Prayer

A breaking when I want to be made whole.
Physically kneeling to find my heart has me
Arms crossed in defiance, in defeat.
Silence when the speaking happens.
My answers are turned into questions
And questions turned into answers.
Stillness and rest. Just being beside
A close friend, or family member no
Longer around for conversation.

Tyler Scott
2014

"Give thanks to the Lord, call on His name." –Psalm 105:1

A Father's Prayer

MAR 3 - 1980 6:50 AM
Dear God please
look after me +
my family + loved ones

I know you are
with us + a great
almighty God + supreme
being over all man
kind i trust in you
+ thanks for all
the blessings you
have bestowed upon me
+ my family thank you
God. you are great. Amen

Written by my father Joe W. Killen March 3, 1980 6:50 am

Bill Killen

Creed

I will find my soul's satisfaction in God
By God's will through Christ's cross,

Or

I will lose all else that lies, waiting in me
By my will through Christ's cross.

Tyler Scott
2014

"Give thanks to the Lord, call on His name." –Psalm 105:1

A Dog's Prayer

Heal me Lord. Heal me Father.
My ears too deaf. My tongue too loose.
My arms too defiant.   My life too dead.

Heal me Lord. Heal me Father.
Your presence calms and corrects.
Let me breathe it all fill my head like menthol

Heal me Lord. Heal me Father.
Yes, a dog barking, pulling
Pulling against you hard.

Heel me Lord. Heal me Father.
Tell me to heel. Tell me to walk
At your side. Let me hear your voice.

Heel me Lord Heal me Father
With your voice let it fill my head
Fill my head like menthol.

Tyler Scott
September, 2016

The Final Inspection

"The Soldier stood and faced God,
Which must always come to pass.
He hoped his shoes were shining,
 just as brightly as his brass.

"Step forward now, you Soldier
How shall I deal with you
Have you always turned the other cheek?
to My Church have you been true"?

The soldier squared his shoulders and
said, "No, Lord, I guess I ain't.
Because those of us who carry guns,
can't always be a saint.

I've had to work most Sundays,
and at times my talk was tough.
And sometimes I've been violent,
because the world is awfully rough.

"Give thanks to the Lord, call on His name." –Psalm 105:1

But, I never took a penny,
that wasn't mine to keep...
Though I worked a lot of overtime,
when the bills got just too steep.

And I never passed a cry for help,
though at times I shook with fear.
And sometimes, God, forgive me,
I've wept unmanly tears.

I know I don't deserve a place,
among the people here.
They never wanted me around,
except to calm their fears

If you've a place for me here, Lord,
it needn't be so grand.
I never expected or had too much,
but if you don't, I'll understand.

There was a silence all around the throne,
where the saints had often trod.
As the Soldier waited quietly,
for the judgment of his God.

"Step forward now, you Soldier,
you've borne your burdens well.
Walk peacefully on Heaven's streets,
you've done your time in Hell."
To all that serve.

-Part II

I'm very saddened by America today,
when they take credit for what others say.

I wrote a poem because of problems in my past,
How was I to know that it was going to last.

It has been read by all and loved the same,
but indeed, at the end there is no name.

The name is simple for those who know,
it's not Kilmer, Longfellow, Service or Poe.

"Give thanks to the Lord, call on His name." –Psalm 105:1

It's a soldier who has fought for his country so true,
he's proud of the ole Red, White and Blue.

You now know the poem the one and the same,
The Final Inspection is the name.

I wrote it because of the trials so true,
and of my buddies who died for country and you.

So, take this poem, take it as you trod,
because in Heaven I'll see my God.

He will look at me and say don't be sad,
others read your poem and you made them glad.

Now step forward my son and look your best,
and come inside with all the rest."

By: Sgt. Joshua Helterbran

Afterglow

I'd like the memory of me to be a happy one,
I'd like to leave an afterglow of smiles when life is done.
I'd like to leave an echo whispering softly down the ways,
Of happy times and laughing times and bright and sunny days.
I'd like the tears of those who grieve, to dry before the sun,
Of happy memories that I leave when life is done.

Funeral Card of Deputy Fire Chief John Eversole
Chicago Fire Department HAZMAT Operations

Fold My Work

Fold my work and lay it away
        For this is the end of a last long day
Out of the clouds have come some tears
        Out of the shadow have come some fears.
Always our Father's loving care,
        And the blessed privilege dear friends and loved ones do not sorrow,
It's good night now,
        But it's good morning tomorrow.

Funeral Card of Past Chief Kurt Eisenschmidt
Riverdale Heights Volunteer Fire Department

"Give thanks to the Lord, call on His name." –Psalm 105:1

The Bell: I Know Who I Am
Distributed by email - Author unknown

I am God's child (John 1:12)
I am Christ's friend (John 15:15)
I am united with the Lord (1 Cor. 6:17)
I am bought with a price (1 Cor. 6:19-20)
I am a saint (set apart for God). (Eph. 1:1)
I am a personal witness of Christ (Acts 1:8)
I am the salt & light of the earth (Matt.5:13-14)
I am a member of the body of Christ (1 Cor 12:27)
I am free forever from condemnation (Rom. 8: 1-2)
I am a citizen of Heaven. I am significant (Phil.3:20)
I am free from any charge against me (Rom. 8:31-34)
I am a minister of reconciliation for God(2 Cor.5:17-21)
I have access to God through the Holy Spirit (Eph. 2:18)
I am seated with Christ in the heavenly realms (Eph. 2:6)
I cannot be separated from the love of God(Rom.8:35-39)
I am established, anointed, sealed by God (2 Cor.1:21-22)
I am assured all things work together for good (Rom. 8: 28)
I have been chosen and appointed to bear fruit (John 15:16)
I may approach God with freedom and confidence (Eph. 3: 12)
I can do all things through Christ who strengthens me (Phil. 4:13)
I am the branch of the true vine, a channel of His life (John 15: 1-5)
I am God's temple (1 Cor. 3: 16). I am complete in Christ (Col. 2: 10)
I am hidden with Christ in God (Col. 3:3). I have been justified (Romans 5:1)
I am God's co-worker (1 Cor. 3:9; 2 Cor 6:1). I am God's workmanship (Eph. 2:10)
I am confident that the good works God has begun in me will be perfected (Phil 1: 5)
I have been redeemed and forgiven (Col. 1:14).
I have been adopted as God's child (Eph 1:5)

I belong to God. Do you know who you are?

"Give thanks to the Lord, call on His name." –Psalm 105:1

Home at Last

When I die, don't weep for me, for I'll be where you'd like to be.
Away from all the pain and strife, that ever haunts us in this life.
I'd like no mourning at my shroud, just a sign to say "no tears allowed."
For I've gone through heaven's gate, and though you tarry, I'll still wait.

Yes, shed no tears, for I have passed, to claim a perfect life at last.
You know my faults, at least in part, you know my independent heart.
No, shed no tears, for there I'll be, with friends who've gone ahead of me.
And when they ask of you I'll say, "You'll be along another day."
No, don't feel sad, I'm home at last; all tears and trials are in the past.

Help finish what I've left undone, it seems so much – I'd just begun.
So, bow your head, and in prayer rejoice, in hymns of praise lift up your voice.
And thank the Lord for wondrous grace, that He gave me entrance to this place.
Yes, I'll be waiting inside the gate. No, don't be sad. You come… I'll wait.

Funeral Card of Colleen Henry

A minute with God
I spent a minute and hope you will too.

With what is going on in the world these days, Heaven could end up a ghost town.

My name is God. You hardly have time for Me. I love you and will always bless you. I am always with you. I need you to spend 60 seconds of your time with Me today. Don't pray, just praise. Today I want this message to go across the world before midnight. Will you help? Please do not delete it and I'll help you with something that you are in need of.

Just dare Me! A blessing is coming your way. Please drop everything and pass it on. Why are prayers getting smaller, but bars and clubs expanding?

Why is it so easy to worship a celebrity, but very difficult to engage with God? Think about it, are you going to forward this or are you going to ignore it because you think you will get laughed at? Forward this to all your friends. 80% of you won't. God said if you deny me in front of your friends, I will deny you on the Day of Judgment.

When one door closes, God opens two. If God has opened doors for you, send this message to everyone…Forward if God's been good to you! I have!!!

Email from Jim Atkinson
September 16, 2017

"Give thanks to the Lord, call on His name." –Psalm 105:1

Short Stories…

By now those of you who have known me for some time know I love to tell stories, especially those that are entertaining and/or educational. I couldn't think of a better way to begin this Section of Short Stories than to begin with Katherine Hankey's hymn from the United Methodist Hymnal "I love to tell the Story."

> *I love to tell the story of unseen things above,*
> *Of Jesus and His glory, of Jesus and His love.*
> *I love to tell the story, Because I know 'tis true;*
> *It satisfies my longings   As nothing else can do.*
> *I love to tell the story, 'Twill be my theme in glory*
> *To tell the old, old story   of Jesus and His love.*

"I Love to Tell the Story"
Katherine Hankey
The United Methodist Hymnal, No. 156

Only a Quarter...
Distributed by email - Author unknown

Several years ago, a preacher from out-of-state accepted a call to a church in Houston, Texas. Some weeks after he arrived, he had an occasion to ride the bus from his home to the downtown area. When he sat down, he discovered that the driver had accidentally given him a quarter too much change.

As he considered what to do, he thought to himself, "You'd better give the quarter back. It would be wrong to keep it." Then he thought, "Oh, forget it, it's only a quarter. Who would worry about this little amount anyway, the bus company gets too much fare; they will never miss it. Accept it as a 'gift from God' and keep quiet."

When his stop came, he paused momentarily at the door, and then he handed the quarter to the driver and said, "Here, you gave me too much change."

The driver, with a smile, replied, "Aren't you the new preacher in town. I have been thinking a lot lately about going somewhere to worship. I just wanted to see what you would do if I gave you too much change. I'll see you at church on Sunday."

When the preacher stepped off of the bus, he literally grabbed the nearest light pole, held on, and said, "Oh God, I almost sold your Son for a quarter."

"Give thanks to the Lord, call on His name." –Psalm 105:1

Our lives are the only Bible some people will ever read. This is a really scary example of how much people watch us as Christians and will put us to the test!

Always be on guard and remember that you carry the name of Christ on your shoulders when you call yourself "Christian."

I'm glad a friend forwarded this to me as a reminder. God bless you; I hope you are having a wonderful day! The Will of God will never take you to where the Grace of God will not PROTECT you...

What a Wonderful way to Explain It!!!!

A sick man turned to his doctor as he was preparing to leave the examination room and said, "Doctor, I am afraid to die, tell me what lies on the other side."

Very quietly, the doctor said, "I don't know."

"You don't know? You, a Christian man, do not know what is on the other side?"

The doctor was holding the handle of the door; on the other side came a sound of scratching and whining and as he opened the door, a dog sprang into the room and leaped on him with an eager show of gladness.

Turning to the patient, the doctor said, "Did you notice my dog?

He's never been in this room before. He didn't know what was inside.

He knew nothing except that his master was here and when the door opened, he sprang in without fear.

I know little of what is on the other side of death, but I do know one thing... I know my Master is there and that is enough."

"Give thanks to the Lord, call on His name." –Psalm 105:1

You Took My Parking Space at Church, this should wake us up.

One day, a man went to visit a church. He got there early, parked his car and got out.

Another car pulled up near him. The driver got out and said, 'Hey, I always park there! You took my place!'

The visitor went inside for Sunday School, found an empty seat and sat down. A young lady from the church approached him and stated, 'That's my seat! You took my place!'

The visitor was somewhat distressed by this rude welcome, but said nothing.

After Sunday School, the visitor went into the sanctuary and sat down. Another member walked up to him and said, 'That's where I always sit! You took my place!'

The visitor was even more troubled by this treatment, but still He said nothing.

Later as the congregation was praying for Christ to dwell among them, the visitor stood up, and his appearance began to change. Horrible scars became visible on his hands and on his sandaled feet. Someone from the congregation noticed him and called out, 'What happened to you' The visitor replied, as his hat became a crown of thorns, and a tear fell from his eye, 'I took your place.'

Daddy's Empty Chair
Distributed by email - Author unknown

A man's daughter had asked the local minister to come and pray with her father.

When the minister arrived, he found the man lying in bed with his head propped up on two pillows.

An empty chair sat beside his bed. The minister assumed that the old fellow had been informed of his visit. "I guess you were expecting me, he said.

'No, who are you" said the father. The minister told him his name and then remarked," I saw the empty chair and I figured you knew I was going to show up."

"Give thanks to the Lord, call on His name." –Psalm 105:1

"Oh yeah, the chair," said the bedridden man. "Would you mind closing the door?"

Puzzled, the minister shut the door.

"I have never told anyone this, not even my daughter," said the man, "But all of my life I have never known how to pray. At church, I used to hear the pastor talk about prayer, but it went right over my head."

I abandoned any attempt at prayer," the old man continued," until one day four years ago, my best friend said to me," Johnny, prayer is just a simple matter of having a conversation with Jesus.

Here is what I suggest. "Sit down in a chair; place an empty chair in front of you, and in faith see Jesus on the chair.

It's not spooky because he promised, 'I will be with you always'. "Then just speak to him in the same way you're doing with me right now."

"So, I tried it and I've liked it so much that I do it a couple of hours every day. I'm careful though. If my daughter saw me talking to an empty chair, she'd either have a nervous breakdown or send me off to the funny farm."

The minister was deeply moved by the story and encouraged the old man to continue on the journey. Then he prayed with him, anointed him with oil and returned to the church.

Two nights later the daughter called to tell the minister that her daddy had died that afternoon.

Did he die in peace?" he asked.

Yes, when I left the house about two o'clock, he called me over to his bedside, told me he loved me and kissed me on the cheek.

When I got back from the store an hour later, I found him.

But there was something strange about his death. Apparently, just before Daddy died, he leaned over and rested his head on the chair beside the bed.

What do you make of that?"

The minister wiped a tear from his eye and said, "I wish we could all go like that."

Prayer is one of the best free gifts we receive.

"Give thanks to the Lord, call on His name." –Psalm 105:1

Spring Cleaning...
Church Bulletin April 18, 1976

God knocked at the door of my heart one day and I looked for a place to hide;
My soul was cluttered and choked with debris and things were untidy inside.

I needed some time to put matters right, surprised He would call on me;
My soul needed cleaning from bottom to top, there were things He should not see.

There were things neglected, long overdue, cobwebs to be brushed from the wall;
Rugs to be shaken and windows cleaned up— I had not expected HIs call.

I stood with my hand on the latch of the door and gazed at the mess in the room
When I opened the door, my soul blushed to see, God had left on my doorstep a broom for me.

University Baptist Church
Orlando, Florida

'Excuse me, are you Jesus?'
Distributed by email - Author unknown

A few years ago, a group of salesmen went to a regional sales convention in Chicago. They had assured their wives that they would be home in plenty of time for Friday night's dinner.

In their rush, with tickets and briefcases, one of these salesmen inadvertently kicked over a table which held a display of apples.

Apples flew everywhere. Without stopping or looking back, they all managed to reach the plane in time for their nearly missed boarding.

ALL BUT ONE!!! He paused, took a deep breath, got in touch with his feelings, and experienced a twinge of compassion for the girl whose apple stand had been overturned. He told his buddies to go on without him, waved good-bye, told one of them to call his wife when they arrived at their home destination and explain his taking a later flight.

Then he returned to the terminal where the apples were all over the terminal floor. He was glad he did.

"Give thanks to the Lord, call on His name." –Psalm 105:1

The 16-year-old girl was totally blind! She was softly crying, tears running down her cheeks in frustration, and at the same time helplessly groping for her spilled produce as the crowd swirled about her, no one stopping and no one to care for her plight.

The salesman knelt on the floor with her, gathered up the apples, put them back on the table and helped organize her display. As he did this, he noticed that many of them had become battered and bruised; these he set aside in another basket. When he had finished, he pulled out his wallet and said to the girl, "Here, please take this $40 for the damage we did."

"Are you okay?" She nodded through her tears. He continued on with, "I hope we didn't spoil your day too badly." As the salesman started to walk away, the bewildered blind girl called out to him, "Mister..." He paused and turned to look back into those blind eyes.

She continued, "Are you Jesus?"

He stopped in mid-stride, and he wondered. Then slowly he made his way to catch the later flight with that question burning and bouncing about in his soul: 'Are you Jesus?'

Do people mistake you for Jesus? That's our destiny, is it not? To be so much like Jesus that people cannot tell the difference as we live and interact with a world that is blind to His love, life and grace.

If we claim to know Him, we should live, walk and act as He would. Knowing Him is more than simply quoting Scripture and going to church. It's actually living the Word as life unfolds day to day.

You are the apple of His eye even though we, too, have been bruised by a fall.

He stopped what He was doing and picked you and me up on a hill called Calvary and paid in full for our damaged fruit.

Editor's Note:

This story is fiction and based on the song "Excuse me are you Jesus" by The Nelons, an award-winning gospel group and 2016 inductees in the Gospel Music Association Gospel Music Hall of Fame.

"Give thanks to the Lord, call on His name." –Psalm 105:1

Sand and Stone
Distributed by email - Author unknown

Two friends were walking through the desert. During some point of the journey, they had an argument; and one friend slapped the other one in the face.

The one who got slapped was hurt, but without saying anything, wrote in the sand, "Today my best friend slapped me in the face."

They kept on walking, until they found an oasis, where they decided to take a bath. The one who had been slapped got stuck in the mire and started drowning, but the friend saved him.

After he recovered from the near drowning, he wrote on a stone: "Today my best friend saved my life".

The friend who had slapped and saved his best friend asked him, "After I hurt you, you wrote in the sand and now, you write on a stone, Why

The friend replied "When someone hurts us we should write it down in sand, where winds of forgiveness can erase it away."

But, when someone does something good for us, we must engrave it in stone where no wind can ever erase it."

Learn to write your hurts in the sand and to carve your blessings in stone.

Bring Potato Chips

A little boy wanted to meet God. He knew it was a long trip to where God lived, So, he packed his suitcase with a bag of potato chips and a six-pack of root beer and started his journey.

When he had gone about three blocks, he met an old man. He was sitting in the park, just staring at some pigeons. The boy sat down next to him and opened his suitcase. He was about to take a drink from his root beer when he noticed that the old man looked hungry, so he offered him some chips. He gratefully accepted It and smiled at him.

His smile was so pretty that the boy wanted to see it again, so he offered him a root beer. Again, he smiled at him. The boy was delighted! They sat there all afternoon eating and smiling, but they never said a word...

"Give thanks to the Lord, call on His name." –Psalm 105:1

As twilight approached, the boy realized how tired he was and he got up to leave; But before he had gone more than a few steps, he turned around, ran back to the old man, and gave him a hug. He gave him his biggest smile ever...

When the boy opened the door to his own house a short time later, his mother was surprised by the look of joy on his face. She asked him, "What did you do today that made you so happy?"

He replied, "I had lunch with God." But before his mother could respond, he added, "You know what? He's got the most beautiful smile I've ever seen!"

Meanwhile, the old man, also radiant with joy, returned to his home. His son was stunned by the look of peace on his face and he asked, "Dad, what did you do today that made you so happy?"

He replied "I ate potato chips in the park with God."

However, before his son responded, he added, "You know, he's much younger than I expected."

Too often we underestimate the power of a touch, a smile, a kind word, a listening ear, an honest compliment, or the smallest act of caring, all of which have the potential to turn a life around.

> **People come into our lives for a reason, a season, or a lifetime! Embrace all equally! Have lunch with God .... bring potato chips**

Email from John Stapleton
December 25, 2015

"Give thanks to the Lord, call on His name." –Psalm 105:1

When You Find a Penny
Distributed by email - Author unknown

You always hear the usual stories of pennies on the sidewalk being good luck, gifts from angels, etc. This is the first time I've ever heard this twist on the story, it gives you something to think about. Several years ago, a friend of mine and her husband were invited to spend the weekend at the husband's employer's home. My friend, Arlene, was nervous about the weekend. The boss was very wealthy, with a fine home on the waterway, and cars costing more than her house.

The first day and evening went well, and Arlene was delighted to have this rare glimpse into how the very wealthy live. The husband's employer was quite generous as a host, and took them to the finest restaurants. Arlene knew she would never have the opportunity to indulge in this kind of extravagance again, so was enjoying herself immensely.

As the three of them were about to enter an exclusive restaurant that evening, the boss was walking slightly ahead of Arlene and her husband. He stopped suddenly, looking down on the pavement for a long, silent moment.

Arlene wondered if she was supposed to pass him. There was nothing on the ground except a single darkened penny that someone had dropped, and a few cigarette butts. Still silent, the man reached down and picked up the penny.

He held it up and smiled, then put it in his pocket as if he had found a great treasure. How absurd! What need did this man have for a single penny? Why would he even take the time to stop and pick it up?

Throughout dinner, the entire scene nagged at her, finally, she could stand it no longer. She causally mentioned that her daughter once had a coin collection, and asked if the penny he had found had been of some value.

A smile crept across the man's face as he reached into his pocket for the penny and held it out for her to see. She had seen many pennies before! What was the point of this?

"Look at it." He said. "Read what it says." She read the words "United States of America."

"No, not that; read further." "One cent" she said.

"No, keep reading." He replied "In God We Trust" she said and he replied "Yes,"

"And?" she asked.

"And if I trust in God, the name of God is holy, even on a coin. Whenever I find a
"Give thanks to the Lord, call on His name." –Psalm 105:1

coin I see that inscription. It is written on every single United States coin, but we never seem to notice it! God drops a message right in front of me telling me to trust Him. Who am I to pass it by?

When I see a coin, I pray, I stop to see if my trust IS in God at that moment. I pick the coin up as a response to God; that I do trust in Him. For a short time, at least, I cherish it as if it were gold. I think it is God's way of starting a conversation with me.

Lucky for me, God is patient and pennies are plentiful. When I was out shopping today, I found a penny on the sidewalk. I stopped and picked it up, and realized that I had been worrying and fretting in my mind about things I cannot change. I read the words, "In God We Trust," and had to laugh, Yes, God, I got the message. It seems that I have been finding an inordinate number of pennies in the last few months, but the pennies are plentiful and God is patient. Have a blessed day. Anonymous.

The Coal Basket Bible
Distributed by email - Author unknown

The story is told of an old man who lived on a farm in the mountains of Kentucky with his young grandson. Each morning, Grandpa was up early sitting at the kitchen table reading from his old worn out Bible.

His grandson who wanted to be just like him tried to imitate him in any way he could.

One day the grandson asked, "Papa, I try to read the Bible just like you but I don't understand it, and what I do understand I forget as soon as I close the book. What good does reading the Bible do?" The Grandfather quietly turned from putting coal in the stove and said, "Take this coal basket down to the river and bring back a basket of water."

The boy did as he was told, even though all the water leaked out before he could get back to the house.

The grandfather laughed and said, "You will have to move a little faster next time." and sent him back to the river with the basket to try again. This time the boy ran faster, but again the basket was empty before he returned home.

Out of breath, he told his grandfather that it was "impossible to carry water in a basket," and he went to get a bucket instead. The old man said, "I don't want a bucket of water; I want a basket of water. You can do this. You're just not trying hard enough," and he went out the door to watch the boy try again.

"Give thanks to the Lord, call on His name." —Psalm 105:1

At this point, the boy knew it was impossible, but he wanted to show his grandfather that even if he ran as fast as he could, the water would leak out before he got very far. The boy scooped the water and ran hard, but when he reached his grandfather the basket was again empty.

Out of breath, he said, "See Papa, it's useless!" "So, you think it is useless?" The old man said, "Look at the basket." The boy looked at the basket and for the first time he realized that the basket looked different. Instead of a dirty old coal basket, it was clean. "Son, that's what happens when you read the Bible. You might not understand or remember everything, but when you read it, it will change you from the inside out."

That is the work of God in our lives. It will change us from the inside out and to slowly transform us into the image of His son. Take time to read a portion of God's word each day, and remind a friend by sharing this story.

"Live Simply, Love Generously, Care Deeply, Speak Kindly, and Leave the Rest to God"

Saying Grace in a Restaurant.

Last week, I took my children to a restaurant. My six-year-old son asked if he could say grace.

As we bowed our heads he said, "God is good, God is great. Thank you for the food, and I would even thank you more if Mom gets us ice cream for dessert. And liberty and justice for all! Amen!"

Along with the laughter from the other customers nearby, I heard a woman remark, "That's what's wrong with this country. Kids today don't even know how to pray. Asking God for ice cream! Why, I never!"

Hearing this, my son burst into tears and asked me, "Did I do it wrong? Is God mad at me?"

As I held him and assured him that he had done a terrific job, and God was certainly not mad at him, an elderly gentleman approached the table.

"Give thanks to the Lord, call on His name." –Psalm 105:1

He winked at my son and said, "I happen to know that God thought that was a great prayer."

"Really" my son asked.

"Cross my heart," the man replied.

Then, in a theatrical whisper, he added (indicating the woman whose remark had started this whole thing), "Too bad she never asks God for ice cream. A little ice cream is good for the soul sometimes."

Naturally, I bought my kids ice cream at the end of the meal. My son stared at his for a moment, and then did something I will remember the rest of my life.

He picked up his sundae and, without a word, walked over and placed it in front of the woman. with a big smile he told her, "Here, this is for you. Ice cream is good for the soul sometimes; and my soul is good already."

Billy Graham's Suit
Distributed by email - Author unknown

In January 2000, leaders in Charlotte, North Carolina, invited their favorite son, Billy Graham, to a luncheon in his honor. Billy initially hesitated to accept the invitation because he struggles with Parkinson's disease. But the Charlotte leaders said, "We don't expect a major address. Just come and let us honor you." So, he agreed.

After wonderful things were said about him, Dr. Graham stepped to the rostrum, looked at the crowd, and said, "I'm reminded today of Albert Einstein, the great physicist who this month has been honored by Time magazine as the Man of the Century.

Einstein was once traveling from Princeton on a train when the conductor came down the aisle, punching the tickets of every passenger. When he came to Einstein, Einstein reached in his vest pocket. He couldn't find his ticket, so he reached in his trouser pockets. It wasn't there, so he looked in his briefcase but couldn't find it. Then he looked in the seat beside him. He still couldn't find it.

The conductor said, "Dr. Einstein, I know who you are. We all know who you are. I'm sure you bought a ticket. Don't worry about it." Einstein nodded appreciatively. The conductor continued down the aisle punching tickets. As he was ready to move to the next car, he turned around and saw the great physicist down on his hands and knees looking under his seat for his ticket.

"Give thanks to the Lord, call on His name." –Psalm 105:1

The conductor rushed back and said, "Dr. Einstein, Dr. Einstein, don't worry, I know who you are. No problem. You don't need a ticket. I'm sure you bought one." Einstein looked at him and said, "Young man, I too, know who I am. What I don't know is where I'm going.'"

Having said that Billy Graham continued, "See the suit I'm wearing It's a brand-new suit. My wife, my children, and my grandchildren are telling me I've gotten a little slovenly in my old age. I used to be a bit more fastidious. So, I went out and bought a new suit for this luncheon and one more occasion. You know what that occasion is? This is the suit in which I'll be buried. But when you hear I'm dead, I don't want you to immediately remember the suit I'm wearing. I want you to remember this: I not only know who I am, I also know where I'm going."

Semper Fi Brother!
Distributed by email - Author unknown

A United States marine was attending some college courses between assignments. He had completed missions in Iraq and Afghanistan. One of the courses had a professor who was an avowed atheist and a member of the ACLU.

One day the professor shocked the class when he came in. He looked to the ceiling and flatly stated, "God, if you are real, then I want you to knock me off this platform. I'll give you exactly 15 minutes." The lecture room fell silent. You could hear a pin drop.

Ten minutes went by and the professor proclaimed, "Here I am God. I'm still waiting."

It got down to the last couple of minutes when the marine got out of his chair, went up to the professor, and cold-cocked him knocking him off the platform. The professor was out cold. The marine went back to his seat and sat there, silently. The other students were shocked and stunned and sat there looking on in silence.

The professor eventually came to, noticeably shaken, looked at the marine and asked, "What the world is the matter with you? Why did you do that?"

The marine calmly replied, "God was too busy today protecting America's troops who are protecting your right to say stupid things and act like an imbecile. ....So, He sent me."

"Give thanks to the Lord, call on His name." –Psalm 105:1

Christian One Liners...

Don't let your worries get the best of you; remember, Moses started out as a basket case.

God Himself does not propose to judge a man until he is dead. So why should you?

Some people are kind, polite, and sweet-spirited until you try to sit in their pews.

Many folks want to serve God, but only as advisers.

It is easier to preach ten sermons than it is to live one.

When you get to your wit's end, you'll find God lives there.

People are funny; they want the front of the bus, middle of the road, and back of the church.

The good Lord didn't create anything without a purpose, but mosquitoes come close.

Opportunity may knock once, but temptation bangs on the front door forever.

Quit griping about your church; if it was perfect, you couldn't belong.

If a church wants a better pastor, it only needs to pray for the one it has.

God made man before woman so as to give him time to think of an answer for her first question.

"Give thanks to the Lord, call on His name." –Psalm 105:1

We're called to be witnesses, not lawyers or judges.

Some minds are like concrete, thoroughly mixed up and permanently set.

"Don't be afraid to try something new. An amateur built the Ark, professionals built the Titanic.

Remember when the funniest jokes were the clean ones? They still are!

I don't know why some people change churches; what difference does it make which one you stay home from?

Peace starts with a smile.

A lot of church members singing 'Standing on the Promises' are just sitting on the premises.

Be ye fishers of men. You catch 'em - He'll clean 'em.

Stop, Drop, and Roll won't work in Hell.

Coincidence is when God chooses to remain anonymous.

Don't put a question mark where God put a period.

Don't wait for 6 strong men to take you to church.

Forbidden fruits create many jams.

God doesn't call the qualified, He qualifies the called.

God grades on the cross, not the curve.

God loves everyone, but probably prefers 'fruits of the spirit' over 'religious nuts!'

"Give thanks to the Lord, call on His name." –Psalm 105:1

God promises a safe landing, not a calm passage.

He who angers you, controls you!

If God is your Co-pilot, swap seats!

Prayer: Don't give God instructions, just report for duty!

The task ahead of us is never as great as the Power behind us.

The Will of God never takes you to where the Grace of God will not protect you.

We don't change the message; the message changes us.

You can tell how big a person is by what it takes to discourage him.

When you forgive you heal. When you let go you grow.

In a world where you can be anything, be kind.

Forgiveness does not change the past but it does enlarge the future.

Remember...Just going to church doesn't make you a Christian any more than standing in your garage makes you a car.

Be kinder than necessary because everyone you meet is fighting some kind of battle"

The best mathematical equation I have ever seen:

$$\frac{1 \text{ cross} + 3 \text{ nails}}{= 4 \text{ given}}$$

"A cheerful heart is good medicine." **Prov. 17:22**

"Give thanks to the Lord, call on His name." –Psalm 105:1

Kids...

Untimely Answered Prayer

During the minister's prayer one Sunday, there was a loud whistle from one of the back pews.

Tommy's mother was horrified. She pinched him into silence and, after church, asked, "Tommy, whatever made you do such a thing?"

Tommy answered, soberly, "I asked God to teach me to whistle, and He did!"

Time to Pray

A pastor asked a little boy if he said his prayers every night. "Yes, sir," the boy replied. "And, do you always say them in the morning, too?" the pastor asked.

"No sir," the boy replied. "I ain't scared in the daytime."

Amen - All Girls

When my daughter, Kelli, said her bedtime prayers, she would bless every family member, every friend, and every animal (current and past). For several weeks, after we had finished the nightly prayer, Kelli would say, "And all girls." This soon became part of her nightly routine, to include this closing. My curiosity got the best of me and I asked her, "Kelli, why do you always add the part about all girls?"

Her response, "Because everybody always finishes their prayers by saying All Men'!"

Say A Prayer

Little Johnny and his family were having Sunday dinner at his Grandmother's house. Everyone was seated around the table as the food was being served. When Little Johnny received his plate, he started eating right away.

"Johnny! Please wait until we say our prayer." said his mother. "I don't need to," the boy replied. "Of course, you do," his mother insisted. "We always say a prayer before eating at our house." "That's at our house," Johnny explained. "But this is Grandma's house and she knows how to cook!"

"Give thanks to the Lord, call on His name." –Psalm 105:1

The Ring Bear

A little boy was in a relative's wedding. As he was coming down the aisle, HE WOULD TAKE TWO STEPS, STOP, AND TURN TO THE CROWD. While facing the crowd, he would put his hands up like claws and roar. So it went, step, step, ROAR, step, step, ROAR, all the way down the aisle.

As you can imagine, the crowd was near tears from laughing so hard by the time he reached the pulpit.

When asked what he was doing, the child sniffed and said, "I was being the Ring Bear".

Prayer Request

One Sunday in a Midwest City, a young child was "acting Up" during the morning worship hour. The parents did their best to maintain some sense of order in the pew but were losing the battle.   Finally, the father picked the little fellow up and walked sternly up the aisle on his way out. Just before reaching the safety of the foyer, the little one called loudly to the congregation, "Pray for me! Pray for me!"

Trash Baskets

One particular four-year-old prayed, "and forgive us our trash baskets as we forgive whose who put trash in in our baskets.

Quiet in Church

A Sunday School teacher asked her little children, as they were on the way to church service, "And why is it necessary to be quiet in church?" One bright little girl replied, "Because people are sleeping."

Old Leaf

A little boy opened the big and old family Bible with fascination, looking at the old pages as he turned them. Then something fell out of the Bible. He picked it up and looked at it closely. It was an old leaf from a tree that has been pressed in between the pages. "Mama, look what I found," the boy called out... "What have you got there, dear?" his mother asked He picked it up and looked at it closely. It was an old leaf from a tree that has been pressed in between the pages.

With astonishment in the young boy's voice he answered, "It's Adam's suit".

"Give thanks to the Lord, call on His name." –Psalm 105:1

Wired

The preacher was wired for sound with a lapel mike, and as he preached, he moved briskly about the platform, jerking the mike cord as he went. Then he moved to one side, getting wound up in the cord and nearly tripping before jerking it again. After several circles and jerks, a little girl in the third pew leaned toward her mother and whispered," If he gets loose, will he hurt us?"

Standing by the door

Six-year old Angie, and her four-year old brother, Joel, were sitting together in church. Joel giggled, sang and talked out loud. Finally, his big sister had had enough. "You're not supposed to talk out loud in church."

"Why? Who's going to stop me?" Joel asked. Angie pointed to the back of the church and said, "See those two men standing by the door? They're hushers."

Which Virgin?

A ten-year old, under the tutelage of her grandmother, was becoming quite knowledgeable about the Bible. Then, one day, she floored her grandmother by asking, "Which Virgin was the mother of Jesus? The virgin Mary or the King James Virgin?"

Cleanin' Chickens

"Late again," the third-grade teacher said to little Sammy.

"It ain't my fault, Miss Crabtree. You can blame this on my Daddy. The reason I'm three hours late is Daddy sleeps naked!"

Now Miss Crabtree had taught grammar school for thirty-some-odd years. So, she asked little Sammy what he meant by that, despite her mounting fears.

Full of grins and mischief, and in the flower of his youth, little Sammy and trouble were old friends, but he always told the truth.

"You see, Miss Crabtree, at the ranch we got this here lowdown coyote. The last few nights he done et six hens and killed Ma's best milk goat.

And last night, when Daddy heard a noise out in the chicken pen, he grabbed his gun and said to Ma, 'that coyote's back again, I'm a gonna git him!'"

"Give thanks to the Lord, call on His name." –Psalm 105:1

'Stay back, he yelled to all us kids!' He was naked as a jaybird, no boots, no pants, no shirt!

To the hen house he crawled, just like an Injun on the snoop. Then he stuck that double barrel through the window of the coop.

As he stared into the darkness, with coyotes on his mind, our old hound dog Zeke had done woke up and come sneakin' up behind Daddy. Then we all looked on plumb helpless as old Zeke stuck that cold nose on Daddy's butt.

Miss Crabtree, we been cleanin' chickens since three o'clock this morning!"

~~~~~~~~~

A mother was preparing pancakes for her sons, Kevin 5, and Ryan 3. The boys began to argue over who would get the first pancake.

Their mother saw the opportunity for a moral lesson. "If Jesus were sitting here, He would say, 'Let my brother have the first pancake, I can wait.'

Kevin turned to his younger brother and said, "Ryan, you be Jesus!"

~~~~~~~~~

A father was at the beach with his children when the four-year-old son ran up to him, grabbed his hand, and led him to the shore where a seagull lay dead in the sand.

"Daddy, what happened to him" the son asked. "He died and went to Heaven," the Dad replied. The boy thought a moment and then said, "Did God throw him back down?"

~~~~~~~~~

A wife invited some people to dinner. At the table, she turned to their six-year-old daughter and said, would you like to say the blessing?"

"I wouldn't know what to say," the girl replied. "Just say what you hear Mommy say," the wife answered. The daughter bowed her head and said, "Lord, why on earth did I invite all these people to dinner?"

~~~~~~~~~

Attending a wedding for the first time, a little girl whispered to her mother, "Why is the bride dressed in white?"

"Give thanks to the Lord, call on His name." –Psalm 105:1

Because white is the color of happiness, and today is the happiest day of her life."

The child thought about this for a moment then said, "So why is the groom wearing black?"

Tenth Commandment

A Sunday school class was studying the Ten Commandments. They were ready to discuss the last one. The teacher asked if anyone could tell her what it was. Susie raised her hand, stood tall, and quoted, "Thou shall not take the covers off the neighbor's wife."

~~~~~~~~~~

Three boys are in the school yard bragging about their fathers. The first boy says, "My Dad scribbles a few words on a piece of paper, he calls it a poem, they give him $50."

The second boy says, "That's nothing. My Dad scribbles a few words on piece of paper, he calls it a song, and they give him $100."

The third boy says, "I got you both beat. My Dad scribbles a few words on a piece of paper, he calls it a sermon, and it takes eight people to collect all the money!"

~~~~~~~~~~~

3-year-old Reese: "Our Father, who does art in heaven, Harold is his name. Amen."

A little boy was overheard praying: "Lord, if you can't make me a better boy, don't worry about it. I'm having a real good time like I am."

~~~~~~~~~

"Give thanks to the Lord, call on His name." –Psalm 105:1

After the christening of his baby brother in church, Jason sobbed all the way home in the back seat of the car. His father asked him three times what was wrong.

Finally, the boy replied, "That preacher said he wanted us brought up in a Christian home, and I wanted to stay with you guys."

~~~~~~~~~

I had been teaching my three-year old daughter, Caitlin, the Lord's Prayer for several evenings at bedtime. She would repeat after me the lines from the prayer.

Finally, she decided to go solo. I listened with pride as she carefully enunciated each word, right up to the end of the prayer: "Lead us not into temptation," she prayed, "but deliver us from E-mail.

~~~~~~~~~

A father wanted to read a magazine but was being bothered by his little girl, Madison. She wanted to know what the United States looked like.

Finally, he tore a sheet out of his new magazine on which was printed the map of the country. Tearing it into small pieces, he gave it to Madison and said, go into the other room and see if you can put this together. This will show you our whole country today.

After a few minutes, Madison returned and handed him the map, correctly fitted and taped together.

The father was surprised and asked how she had finished so quickly.

Oh, she said; on the other side of the paper is a picture of Jesus. When I got all of Jesus back where He belonged, then our country just came together.'

~~~~~~~~~

Little Rodney ran into the hospital room excitedly yelling, "Grandpa, Grandpa, make a noise like a frog."

Grandpa replied, "Rodney, why do you want me to make a noise like a frog?"

Rodney replies, "'cause grandma said when you croak we're going to Disney!"

"Give thanks to the Lord, call on His name." –Psalm 105:1

A little girl, dressed in her Sunday best, was running as fast as she could, trying not to be late for Bible class. As she ran she prayed, "Dear Lord, please don't let me be late! Dear Lord, please don't let me be late!"

While she was running and praying, she tripped on a curb and fell, getting her clothes dirty and tearing her dress. She got up, brushed herself off, and started running again! As she ran she once again began to pray" Dear Lord, please don't let me be late...But please don't shove me either!"

~~~~~~~~~~~~~

A Sunday school teacher was discussing the Ten Commandments with her five and six-year olds. After explaining the commandment to "Honor thy father and thy mother," she asked, "Is there a commandment that teaches us how to treat our brothers and sisters?" Without missing a beat, one little boy answered, "Thou shall not kill."

~~~~~~~~~~~~~

At Sunday School, they were teaching how God created everything, including human beings. Little Johnny seemed especially intent when they told him how Eve was created out of one of Adam's ribs. Later in the week his mother noticed him lying down as though he was ill, and she said, "Johnny, what is the matter" Little Johnny responded, "I have pain in my side. I think I'm going to have a wife."

~~~~~~~~~~~~~

Two boys were walking home from Sunday school after hearing a strong preaching on the devil. One said to the other, "What do you think about all this Satan stuff"

The other boy replied, "Well, you know how Santa Claus turned out. It's probably just your Dad."

~~~~~~~~~~~~~

A Sunday School teacher asked her class why Joseph and Mary took baby Jesus with them to Jerusalem. A small child replied, "They couldn't get a baby-sitter."

"Give thanks to the Lord, call on His name." –Psalm 105:1

Palm Sunday

It was Palm Sunday and, because of a sore throat, five-year-old Johnny stayed home from church with a sitter. When the family returned home, they were carrying several palm branches. The boy asked what they were for. "People held them over Jesus' head as walked by," "Wouldn't you know it," the boy fumed, "the one Sunday I don't go, He shows up!"

Children's Sermon

One Easter Sunday morning as the minister was preaching the children's sermon, he reached into his bag of props and pulled out an egg. He pointed at the egg and asked the children, "What's in here?" "I know!" a little boy exclaimed, "Panty hose".

Fifth Grade Assignment: What is God Like?

A fifth-grade teacher in a Christian school asked her class to look at TV commercials and see if they could use them in 20 ways to communicate ideas about God. Here are some of the results:

God is like BAYER ASPIRIN .... He works miracles.
God is like a FORD............. He's got a better idea.
God is like COKE................ He's the real thing.
God is like HALLMARK CARDS.......... He cared enough to send His very best.
God is like. TIDE He gets the stains out others leave behind. ...
God is like. GENERAL ELECTRIC He brings good things to life.
God is like. WAL-MART He has everything.
God is like. ALKA-SELTZER Try Him, you'll like Him
God is like. SCOTCH TAPE You can't see Him, but you know He's there.
God is like. DELTA He's ready when you are.
God is like. ALLSTATE You're in good hands with Him.
God is like. VO-5 Hair Spray; He holds through all kinds of weather
God is like. DIAL SOAP Aren't you glad you have Him? Don't you wish everybody did?
God is like. The US POST OFFICE Neither rain, nor snow, nor sleet nor ice will keep Him from His appointed destination.
God is like. Chevrolet. . .. He is the heartbeat of America
God is like Maxwell House. ..... . Good to the very last drop
God is like Bounty He is the quicker picker upper. Can handle the tough jobs. And He won't fall apart on you
God is like. The Energizer Bunny He Keeps Going, and Going, and Going....

"Give thanks to the Lord, call on His name." –Psalm 105:1

Kid's Version of the Bible

In the beginning, which occurred near the start, there was nothing but God, darkness, and some gas. The Bible says, 'The Lord thy God is one,' but I think He must be a lot older than that. Anyway, God said, 'Give me a light!' and someone did. Then God made the world.

He split the Adam and made Eve. Adam and Eve were naked, but they weren't embarrassed because mirrors hadn't been invented yet. Adam and Eve disobeyed God by eating one bad apple, so they were driven from the Garden of Eden. Not sure what they were driven in though, because they didn't have cars.

Adam and Eve had a son, Cain, who hated his brother as long as he was Abel. Pretty soon all of the early people died off, except for Methuselah, who lived to be like a million or something.

One of the next important people was Noah, who was a good guy, but one of his kids was kind of a ham. Noah built a large boat and put his family and some animals on it. He asked some other people to join him, but they said they would have to take a rain check.

After Noah came Abraham, Isaac, and Jacob. Jacob was more famous than his brother, Esau, because Esau sold Jacob his birthmark in exchange for some pot roast. Jacob had a son named Joseph who wore a really loud sports coat.

Another important Bible guy is Moses, whose real name was Charlton Heston. Moses led the Israel Lights out of Egypt and away from the evil Pharaoh after God sent ten plagues on Pharaoh's people. These plagues included frogs, mice, lice, bowels, and no cable. God fed the Israel Lights everyday with manicotti. Then He gave them His top ten Commandments

These include don't lie, cheat, smoke, dance, or covet your neighbor's bottom (the Bible uses a bad word for bottom that I'm not supposed to say. But my Dad uses it sometimes when he talks about the President). Oh, yeah, I just thought of one more: Humor thy father and thy mother.

One of Moses' best helpers was Joshua who was the first Bible guy to use spies. Joshua fought the battle of Geritol and the fence fell over on the town.

After Joshua came David. He got to be king by killing a giant with a slingshot. He had a son named Solomon who had about 300 wives and 500 porcupines. My teacher says he was wise, but that doesn't sound very wise to me. After Solomon, there were a bunch of major league prophets. One of these was Jonah, who was swallowed by a big whale and then barfed up on the shore.

"Give thanks to the Lord, call on His name." –Psalm 105:1

There were also some minor league prophets, but I guess we don't know much about them.

After the Old Testament came the New Testament. Jesus is the star of the New Testament. He was born in Bethlehem in a barn. I wish I had been born in a barn, too, because my mom is always saying to me, 'Close the door! Were you born in a barn? ' It would be nice to be able to say, 'Yes mom, don't you remember? I was.'

During His life, Jesus had many arguments with sinners like the Pharisees and the Republicans. Jesus also had twelve opossums.

The worst one was Judas Asparagus. Judas was so evil that they named a terrible vegetable after him.

Jesus was a great man. He healed many leopards and even preached to some Germans on the Mount. But the Republicans and all those guys put Jesus on trial before Pontius the Pilot. Pilot didn't stick up for Jesus. He just washed his hands instead.

Anyway, Jesus died for our sins, and then came back to life again. He went up to Heaven but will be back at the end of the Aluminum. His return is foretold in the book of Revolution.

Well, that's pretty much the way I understand it, except I think he got the Republicans and Democrats mixed up.

The Bible According to Kids

The jewels found below are said to be written by actual students and are genuine, authentic, and unreduced—

In the first book of the Bible, Guinesis, God got tired of creating the world, so she took the Sabbath off.

Adam and Eve were created from an apple tree.

Noah's wife was called Joan of Ark. Noah built an ark, which the animals come on to in pears.

Lot's wife was a pillar of salt by day, but a ball of fire by night.

The Jews were a proud people and throughout history they had trouble with the unsympathetic Genitals.

"Give thanks to the Lord, call on His name." –Psalm 105:1

Samson was a strongman who let himself be led astray by a Jezebel like Delilah. Samson slayed the Philistines with the axe of the Apostles.

Moses led the Hebrews to the Red Sea, where they made unleavened bread, which is bread without any ingredients.

The Egyptians were all drowned in the dessert., Afterwards, Moses went up to Mount Cyanide to get the ten amendments.

The first commandment was when Eve told Adam to eat the apple. The fifth commandment is to humor they father and mother. The seventh commandment is thou shall not admit adultery.

Moses died before he ever reached Canada. Then Joshua led the Hebrews in the battle of geritol. The greatest miracle in the Bible is when Joshua told his son to stand still and he obeyed him.

David was Hebrew King skilled at playing the liar. He fought with the Finklesteins, a race of people who lived in biblical times.

Solomon, one of David's sons had 300 wives and 700 porcupines.

When Mary heard that she was the mother of Jesus, she sang the Magna Carta.

Jesus enunciated the Golden Rule, which says to do one to others before they do one to you. He also explained, a man doth not live by sweat alone.

It was a miracle when Jesus rose from the dead and managed to get the tombstone off the entrance.

The people who fooled the Lord were called the 12 decibels.

The epistles were the wives of the apostles.

One of the possums was St. Mathew who was also a taximan.

St. Paul cavorted to Christianity. He preached holy acrimony, which is another name for marriage.

A Christian should have only one spouse. This is called monotony.

Michael Merwick
December, 1998

"Give thanks to the Lord, call on His name." –Psalm 105:1

First Time Ushers

A little boy in church for the first time watched as the ushers passed around the offering plates. When they came near his pew, the boy said loudly, "Don't pay for me, Daddy, I'm under five."

Climb the Walls

"Oh, I sure am happy to see you," the little boy said to his grandmother on his mother's side. "Now maybe daddy will do the trick he has been promising us." The grandmother was curious, "What trick is that?" she asked. "I heard him tell mommy that he would climb the walls if you came to visit," the little boy answered.

The Water Pistol

When my three-year-old son opened the birthday gift from his grandmother he discovered a water pistol. He squealed with delight and headed for the nearest sink. I was not so pleased. I turned to mom and said, "I'm surprised at you. Don't you remember how we used to drive you crazy with water guns?" Mom smiled and then replied…." I remember!"

Pop Pop How old are you?

Granddaughter: Pop Pop, how old are you?

Pop Pop: I will be 64 on my next birthday.

Granddaughter: I bet you remember when the Dead Sea was sick.

Grandma's Age

Little Johnny asked his grandma how old she was. Grandma answered "39 and holding." Johnny thought for a moment, and then said," and how old would you be if you let go?"

Alike God

My grandson was visiting one day when he asked, "Grandma, do you know how you and God are alike?" I mentally polished my halo, while I asked, "No, how are we alike?" "You're both old", he replied.

"Give thanks to the Lord, call on His name." –Psalm 105:1

Six reasons not to mess with children

The first day of school, the teacher asked each of her 4th graders what they did for the summer. Mary Jane said she read the Bible from Genesis through Revelations.

The teacher asked Mary Jane what was her favorite story in the Bible, to which she replied," Jonah and the whale. The whale swallowed Jonah."

The teacher said it was physically impossible for a whale to swallow a human because even though it was a very large mammal, its throat was very small.

The little girl stated that Jonah was swallowed by a whale.

Irritated, the teacher reiterated that a whale could not swallow a human; it was physically impossible.

The little girl said, "When I get to heaven I will ask Jonah."

The teacher then asked, "What if Jonah isn't there?"

The little girl replied, "Then you ask him."

Drawing God

A Kindergarten teacher was observing her classroom of children while they were drawing. She would occasionally walk around to see each child's work.

As she got to one little girl who was working diligently, she asked what the drawing was.

The girl replied, "I'm drawing God."

The teacher paused and said, "But no one knows what God looks like."

Without missing a beat, or looking up from her drawing, the girl replied, "They will in a minute."

"Give thanks to the Lord, call on His name." –Psalm 105:1

Class Picture

The children had all been photographed, and the teacher was trying to persuade them each to buy a copy of the group picture.

"Just think how nice it will be to look at it when you are all grown up and say, 'There's Jennifer; she's a lawyer,' or 'That's Michael; he's a doctor.'"

A small voice at the back of the room rang out, "And there's the teacher; she's dead."

~~~~~~~~~

A teacher was giving a lesson on the circulation of the blood. Trying to make the matter clearer, she said, "Now, class, if I stood on my head, the blood, as you know, would run into it, and I would turn red in the face."

"Yes," the class said.

"Then why is it that while I am standing upright in the ordinary position, the blood doesn't run into my feet?".

A little fellow shouted, "Cause your feet ain't empty."

The children were lined up in the cafeteria of a Catholic elementary school for lunch. At the head of the table was a large pile of apples. The nun made a note, and posted on the apple tray:

"Take only ONE. God is watching."

Moving further along the lunch line, at the other end of the table was a large pile of chocolate chip cookies. A child had written a note, "Take all you want. God is watching the apples."

"Give thanks to the Lord, call on His name." –Psalm 105:1

How to get to Heaven

A little boy was waiting for his mother to come out of the grocery store. As he waited, he was approached by a man who asked, "Son, can you tell me where the Post Office is?"

The little boy replied, "Sure! Just go straight down this street a couple blocks and turn to your right."

The man thanked the boy kindly and said, "I'm the new pastor in town. I'd like for you to come to church on Sunday. I'll show you how to get to Heaven."

The little boy replied with a chuckle; "You're kidding me, right?

You don't even know the way to the Post Office!"

Lot's Wife

The Sunday School teacher was describing how Lot's wife looked back and turned into a pillar of salt, when little Jason interrupted, "My Mommy looked back once while she was driving," he announced triumphantly, "and she turned into a telephone pole!"

Good Samaritan

A Sunday school teacher was telling her class the story of the Good Samaritan. She asked the class, 'If you saw a person lying on the roadside, all wounded and bleeding, what would you do?'

A thoughtful little girl broke the hushed silence, 'I think I'd throw up.'

Higher Power

A Sunday school teacher said to her children, "We have been learning how powerful kings and queens were in Bible times. But, there is a Higher Power. Can anybody tell me what it is?"

One child blurted out, "Aces!"

"Give thanks to the Lord, call on His name." –Psalm 105:1

Moses and the Red Sea

Nine-year-old Joey was asked by his mother what he had learned in Sunday School.

'Well, Mom, our teacher told us how God sent Moses behind enemy lines on a rescue mission to lead the Israelites out of Egypt.

When he got to the Red Sea, he had his army build a pontoon bridge and all the people walked across safely. Then he radioed headquarters for reinforcements.

They sent bombers to blow up the bridge and all the Israelites were saved.'

'Now, Joey, is that really what your teacher taught you?' his mother asked.

'Well, no, Mom. But, if I told it the way the teacher did, you'd never believe it!'

The Lord is My Shepherd

A Sunday School teacher decided to have her young class memorize one of the most quoted passages in the Bible - Psalm 23.   She gave the youngsters a month to learn the chapter.

Little Rick was excited about the task - but he just couldn't remember the Psalm. After much practice, he could barely get past the first line.

On the day that the kids were scheduled to recite Psalm 23 in front of the congregation, Ricky was so nervous.

When it was his turn, he stepped up to the microphone and said proudly, 'The Lord is my Shepherd, and that's all I need to know.'

Being Thankful

A Rabbi said to a precocious six-year-old boy, 'So your mother says your prayers for you each night? That's very commendable. What does she say?'   The little boy replied, 'Thank God he's in bed!'

It's nice to be important, but it's important to be nice.

"Give thanks to the Lord, call on His name." –Psalm 105:1

Genealogy

A little girl asked her father, 'How did the human race appear?' The father answered, 'God made Adam and Eve and they had children and so was all mankind made.

'Two days later the girl asked her mother the same question. The mother answered, 'Many years ago there were monkeys from which the human race evolved.

'The confused girl returned to her father and said, 'Dad, how is it possible that you told me the human race was created by God, and Mama said they developed from monkeys?

'The father answered, 'Well, dear, it is very simple. I told you about my side of the family and your Mama told you about hers.'

Did Noah Fish?

A Sunday school teacher asked, "Johnny, do you think Noah did a lot of fishing when he was on the Ark?"

"No," replied Johnny. "How could he, with just two worms?'

"Give thanks to the Lord, call on His name." –Psalm 105:1

Offertory Prayer

*A visiting minister during the offertory prayer:

"Dear Lord," he began with arms extended and a rapturous look on his upturned face, "without you we are but dust..."

He would have continued, but at that moment one very obedient little girl (who was listening carefully for a change!) leaned over to her mother and asked quite audibly in her shrill little girl voice, "Mommy, what is butt dust?"

Died in Service

In the foyer of the church staring up at a large plaque. It was covered with names with small American flags mounted on either side of it.

The seven-year-old had been staring at the plaque for some time, so the pastor walked up, stood beside the little boy, and said quietly, "Good morning Alex."

"Good morning Pastor," he replied, still focused on the plaque. "Pastor what is this?" he asked the pastor.

The pastor said, "Well, son, it's a memorial to all the young men and women who died in the service."

Soberly, they just stood together, staring at the large plaque.

Finally, little Alex's voice, barely audible and trembling with fear, asked, "Which service, the 9:45 or the 11:15?"

"Give thanks to the Lord, call on His name." –Psalm 105:1

Longer Stories

Church Hid in the Weeds
Distributed by email - Author unknown

Just two little boys walking down a dusty lane.....
They came upon this old white house...with broken window panes

The paint was faded, the shine was gone...the grass had grown so high....
still they made their little feet go see what was inside.

They opened up the squeaky door and then it came to light....
This must have been an old church house...once upon a time .

Dirty, dusty wooden pews...a pulpit that still stood...
A Bible laid upon it....though the pages weren't too good.

An offering plate and song books too...were lying on the floor.
They must have left this old church fast..the day they closed these doors.

And over in the corner...a piano was still there.
it must have played a pretty tune..but I guess nobody cared.

So little Bill looked up at Tommy.. and Tommy looked at Bill...
Why don't we clean this old church up, and get these old pews filled?"

They took a rag and wiped the dust...to try and make things shine..
And then they took the offering plate...and put in it their last dime.

They took a broom and swept the floor...and picked up broken glass....
They got it all so nice and neat...and then they mowed the grass.

"Give thanks to the Lord, call on His name." –Psalm 105:1

They lifted up the old church sign... and stood it by a tree...
right down by that old dirt road where everyone could see.

They ran back home, to find Daddy gone but their Momma was inside... Just to find her hurt again...where Daddy had made her cry.

"Don't cry Momma, wipe those tears," Little Bill and Tommy smiled...
"Cause! we have a big surprise for you....just down the road a mile."

Hand in hand they tugged at her.until they made her run....
"What is it Bill, Oh Tommy, just what have you two kids done?"

And then they came upon the house... once hidden by the weeds...
and there it stood a country church... just like it used to be.

"But what is it, Mother? What's with your tears? We thought this would bring you joy."
"Yes, but hush kids now and listen close... my two sweet precious boys."

They both got quiet and stood real still...for the words they heard so true....
was Daddy praying in the church...with his head bowed on the pew.

"Forgive me Lord! Forgive me Lord! though I' m not worthy of Your love...
shine down on this sinner man. sweet Salvation from above."

"For I've been out in the world, You know..living my life all wrong...
until I came upon this church; the place where I belong."

"I never noticed it before... all those times I passed it up..
I guess I wasn't looking, Lord... or maybe I was drunk."

"Bless oh Lord, yes, bless oh Lord...the one who made me see..
this little church that used to hide... behind all those tall weeds."

And then he raised his head and stood... with his hands high in the air...
to find two dirty, tear-faced boys... with Momma standing there.

They ran up to him, hugged him tight... as their tears fell on the floor.
"Don't worry kids, I'm not the Dad, the one you've known before."

Things are different for us now.. so keep on those pretty smiles...
and let's go gather people in... to walk down these church aisles."

Then Bill looked up at Tommy... and Tommy looked at Bill...
"Come on brother, let's get to work... to get these old pews filled."

"Give thanks to the Lord, call on His name." –Psalm 105:1

"For we need no special blessing...for cleaning up this church...
'cause, God gave us back our Daddy... and that's more than gold is worth."

Sunday morning, pews all filled and smiles on every face...
Especially two little country boys... the ones who found this place.

Though it was hid back in the weeds...and so far out of sight...
Nothing's ever hard to find if you're walking toward God's light.

"But if we walk in the light, as He is in the light, we have fellowship with one another, and the blood of Jesus, his Son cleanses us from every sin." **1 John 1:7**

The Tablecloth
Email circulated via internet

The brand-new pastor and his wife, newly assigned to their first ministry, to reopen a church in suburban Brooklyn, arrived in early October excited about their opportunities. When they saw their church, it was very run down and needed much work. They set a goal to have everything done in time to have their first service on Christmas Eve.

They worked hard, repairing pews, plastering walls, painting, etc., and on December 18 were ahead of schedule and just about finished. On December 19, a terrible tempest - a driving rainstorm hit the area and lasted for two days.

On the 21st, the pastor went over to the church. His heart sank when he saw that the roof had leaked, causing a large area of plaster about 20 feet by 8 feet to fall off the front wall of the sanctuary just behind the pulpit, beginning about head high.

The pastor cleaned up the mess on the floor, and not knowing what else to do but postpone the Christmas Eve service, headed home. On the way, he noticed that a local business was having a flea market type sale for charity so he stopped in. One of the items was a beautiful, handmade, ivory colored, crocheted tablecloth with exquisite work, fine colors and a Cross embroidered right in the center. It was just the right size to cover up the hole in the front wall. He bought it and headed back to the church.

By this time, it had started to snow. An older woman running from the opposite direction was trying to catch the bus. She missed it. The pastor invited her to wait in the warm church for the next bus 45 minutes later.

She sat in a pew and paid no attention to the pastor while he got a ladder, hangers, etc., to put up the tablecloth as a wall tapestry. The pastor could hardly believe how beautiful it looked and it covered up the entire problem area.

"Give thanks to the Lord, call on His name." –Psalm 105:1

Then he noticed the woman walking down the center aisle. Her face was like a sheet. "Pastor," she asked, "Where did you get that tablecloth?"

The pastor explained. The woman asked him to check the lower right corner to see if the initials, EBG were crocheted into it there. They were. These were the initials of the woman, and she had made this tablecloth 35 years before, in Austria.

The woman could hardly believe it as the pastor told how he had just gotten the tablecloth. The woman explained that before the war she and her husband were well-to-do people in Austria. When the Nazis came, she was forced to leave. Her husband was going to follow her the next week. She was captured, sent to prison and never saw her husband or her home again.

The pastor wanted to give her the tablecloth; but she made the pastor keep it for the church. The pastor insisted on driving her home, that was the least he could do. She lived on the other side of Staten Island and was only in Brooklyn for the day for a housecleaning job.

What a wonderful service they had on Christmas Eve. The church was almost full. The music and the spirit were great. At the end of the service, the pastor and his wife greeted everyone at the door and many said that they would return.

One older man, whom the pastor recognized from the neighborhood, continued to sit in one of the pews and stare, and the pastor wondered why he wasn't leaving. The man asked him where he got the tablecloth on the front wall because it was identical to one that his wife had made years ago when they lived in Austria before the war and how could there be two tablecloths so much alike.

He told the pastor how the Nazis came, how he forced his wife to flee for her safety, and he was supposed to follow her, but he was arrested and put in a prison. He never saw his wife or his home again all the 35 years in between.

The pastor asked him if he would allow him to take him for a little ride. They drove to Staten Island and to the same house where the pastor had taken the woman three days earlier.

He helped the man climb the three flights of stairs to the woman's apartment knocked on the door and he saw the greatest Christmas reunion he could ever imagine.

This story was posted on the internet January 7, 2009 by John Foresman

"Give thanks to the Lord, call on His name." –Psalm 105:1

Childhood Friend

After a few of the usual Sunday evening hymns, the church's pastor slowly stood up, walked over to the pulpit and before he gave his sermon for the evening, briefly introduced a guest minister who was in the service that evening.

In the introduction, the pastor told the congregation that the guest minister was one of his dearest childhood friends and that he wanted him to have a few moments to greet the church and share whatever he felt would be appropriate for the service. With that, an elderly man stepped to the pulpit and began to speak.

"A father, his son, and a friend of his son were sailing off the pacific coast,", he began. "When a fast approaching storm blocked any attempt to get back to the shore. The waves were so high, that even though the father was an experienced sailor, he could not keep the boat upright and the three were swept into the ocean as the boat capsized."

The old man hesitated for a moment, making eye contact with two teenagers who were, for the first time since the service began, looking somewhat interested in his story. The aged minister continued with his story, "grabbing a rescue line, the father had to make the most excruciating decision of his life: to which boy would he throw the other end of the life line? He only had seconds to make the decision. The father knew that his son was a Christian and he also knew that his son's friend was not.

The agony of his decision could not be matched by the torrent of waves. As the father yelled out, "I love you, son!" He threw out the life line to his son's friend.

By the time the father had pulled the friend back to the capsized boat, his son had disappeared beneath the raging swells into the black of night. His body was never recovered.

By this time, the two teenagers were sitting up straight in the pew, anxiously waiting for the next words to come out of the old minister's mouth.

"The father," he continued, "knew his son would step into eternity with Jesus and he could not bear the thought of his son's friend stepping into an eternity without Jesus, therefore, he sacrificed his son to save the son's friend."

How great is the love of God that He should do the same for us? Our Heavenly Father sacrificed His only begotten Son that we could be saved. I urge you to accept His offer to rescue you and take a hold of the life line He is throwing out to you in this service."

With that, the old man turned and sat back down in his chair as silence filled the room.

"Give thanks to the Lord, call on His name." –Psalm 105:1

The pastor again walked slowly to the pulpit and delivered a brief sermon with an invitation at the end. However, no one responded to the appeal. Within minutes at the service ended, the two teenagers were at the old man's side.

"That was a nice story," politely stated one of them, "But I don't think it was very realistic for a father to give up his only son's life in hopes that the other boy would become a Christian."

"Well, you've got a point there," the old man replied. Glancing down at his worn bible a big smile broadened his narrow face.

He once again looked up at the boys and said, "It sure isn't very realistic, is it? But I'm standing here today to tell you that story gives me a glimpse of what it must have been like for God to give up His son for me.

You see.... I was that father and your pastor is my son's friend."

Don't Forget to Keep your Fork

There was a young woman who had been diagnosed with a terminal illness and had been given three months to live. So, as she was getting her things "in order," she contacted her pastor and had him come to her house to discuss certain aspects of her final wishes.

She told him which hymns she wanted sung at the service, what scriptures she would like read, and what outfit she wanted to be buried in. Everything was in order, and the pastor was preparing to leave, when the young woman suddenly remembered something very important to her.

There's one more thing," she said excitedly. What's that?" came the pastor's reply.

This is very important," the young woman continued. "I want to be buried with a fork in my right hand."

The pastor stood looking at the young woman, not knowing quite what to say. "That surprises you, doesn't it?" the young woman asked.

"Give thanks to the Lord, call on His name." –Psalm 105:1

'Well, to be honest, I'm puzzled by the request," said the pastor.

The young woman explained. "My grandmother once told me this story, and from there on out, I have always done so. I have also always tried to pass along its message to those I love and those who are in need of encouragement. In all my years of attending church socials and potluck dinners, I always remember that when the dishes of the main course were being cleared, someone would inevitably lean over and say, "Keep your fork'.

It was my favorite part because I knew that something better was coming...like velvety chocolate cake or deep-dish apple pie; something wonderful, and with substance!

So, I just want people to see me there in that casket with a fork in my hand, and I want them to wonder 'What's with the fork?' Then, I want you to tell them: 'Keep your fork - the best is yet to come'."

The pastor's eyes welled up with tears! of joy as he hugged the young woman goodbye. He knew this would be one of the last times he would see her before her death. But he also knew that the young woman had a better grasp of heaven than he did. She had a better grasp of what heaven would be like than many people twice her age, with twice as much experience and knowledge. She KNEW that something better was coming.

At the funeral, people were walking by the young woman's casket and they saw the pretty dress she was wearing and the fork placed in her right hand. Over and over, the pastor heard the question "What's with the fork?" And over and over he smiled.

During his message, the pastor told the people of the conversation he had with the young woman shortly before she died. He also told them about the fork and about what it symbolized to her. The pastor told the people how he could not stop thinking about the fork and told them that they probably would not be able to stop thinking about it either. He was right.

So, the next time you reach down for your fork, let it remind you ever so gently, that the best is yet to come.

Friends are a very rare jewel, indeed. They make you smile and encourage you to succeed. They lend an ear, they share a word of praise, and they always want to open their hearts to us.

Cherish the time you have, and the memories you share. Being friends with someone is not an opportunity but a sweet responsibility and don't forget to keep your fork.

"Give thanks to the Lord, call on His name." –Psalm 105:1

Red Marbles
Distributed by email - Author unknown

I was at the corner grocery store buying some early potatoes.

I noticed a small boy, delicate of bone and feature, ragged but clean, hungrily apprizing a basket of freshly picked green peas. I paid for my potatoes, but was also drawn to the display of fresh green peas.

I am a pushover for creamed peas and new potatoes. Pondering the peas, I couldn't help overhearing the conversation between Mr. Miller (the store owner) and the ragged boy next to me.

"Hello Barry, how are you today?"

"H'lo, Mr. Miller. Fine, thank ya. Jus' admirin' them peas. They sure look good."

"They are good, Barry. How's your Ma?" Mr. Miller replied.

"Fine. Gittin' stronger alla' time."

"Good. Anything I can help you with?" Mr. Miller asked.

"No, Sir. Jus' admirin' them peas."

"Would you like to take some home?" asked Mr. Miller.

"No, Sir. Got nuthin' to pay for 'em with."

"Well, what have you to trade me for some of those peas?"

"All I got's my prize marble here"

"Is that right? Let me see I'" said Miller.

"Here 'tis. She's a dandy."

"I can see that. Hmmmmm, only thing is this one is blue and I sort of go for red. Do you have a red one like this at home?" the store owner asked.

"Not zackley but almost." "Tell you what. Take this sack of peas home with you and next trip this way let me look at that red marble", Mr. Miller told the boy.

"Sure will. Thanks Mr. Miller."

"Give thanks to the Lord, call on His name." —Psalm 105:1

Mrs. Miller, who had been standing nearby, came over to help me.

With a smile said, "There are two other boys like him in our community, all three are in very poor circumstances.

Jim just loves to bargain with them for peas, apples, tomatoes, or whatever.

When they come back with their red marbles, and they always do, he decides he doesn't like red after all and he sends them home with a bag of produce for a green marble or an orange one, when they come on their next trip to the store."

I left the store smiling to myself, impressed with this man.

A short time later I moved to Colorado , but I never forgot the story of this man, the boys, and their bartering for marbles.

Several years went by, each more rapid than the previous one.

Just recently I had occasion to visit some old friends in that Idaho community and while I was there learned that Mr. Miller had died.

They were having his visitation that evening and knowing my friends wanted to go, I agreed to accompany them.

Upon arrival at the mortuary we fell into line to meet the relatives of the deceased and to offer whatever words of comfort we could.

Ahead of us in line were three young men.

One was in an army uniform and the other two wore nice haircuts, dark suits and white shirts...all very professional looking.

They approached Mrs. Miller, standing composed and smiling by her husband's casket.

Each of the young men hugged her, kissed her on the cheek, spoke briefly with her and moved on to the casket.

Her misty light blue eyes followed them as, one by one, each young man stopped briefly and placed his own warm hand over the cold pale hand in the casket.

Each left the mortuary awkwardly, wiping his eyes.

Our turn came to meet Mrs. Miller. I told her who I was and reminded her of the story from those many years ago and what she had told me about her husband's bartering for marbles.

"Give thanks to the Lord, call on His name." –Psalm 105:1

7

With her eyes glistening, she took my hand and led me to the casket.

"Those three young men who just left were the boys I told you about. They just told me how they appreciated the things Jim 'traded' them.

Now, at last, when Jim could not change his mind about color or size.... they came to pay their debt.

We've never had a great deal of the wealth of this world," she confided, "but right now, Jim would consider himself the richest man in Idaho."

With loving gentleness she lifted the lifeless fingers of her deceased husband. Resting underneath were three exquisitely shined red marbles.

The Moral: We will not be remembered by our words, but by our kind deeds. Life is not measured by the breaths we take, but by the moments that take our breath.

All the Good Things
Distributed by email October 14, 1997

He was in the first third grade class I taught at Saint Mary's School in Morris, Minnesota. All 34 of my students were dear to me, but Mark Eklund was one in a million. Very neat in appearance, but had that happy-to-be-alive attitude that made even his occasional mischievousness delightful.

Mark talked incessantly. I had to remind him again and again that talking without permission was not acceptable. What impressed me so much, though, was his sincere response every time I had to correct him for misbehaving – "Thank you for correcting me, Sister!" I didn't know what to make of it at first, but before long I became accustomed to hearing it many times a day.

One morning my patience was growing thin when Mark talked once too often, and then I made a novice-teacher's mistake. I looked at him and said, if you say one more word, I am going to tape your mouth shut!

It wasn't ten seconds later when Chuck blurted out, "Mark is talking again." I hadn't asked any of the students to help me watch Mark, but since I had stated the punishment in front of the class, I had to act on it. I remember the scene as if it had occurred this morning. I walked to my desk, very deliberately opened my drawer and took a roll of masking tape. Without saying a word, I proceeded to Mark's desk, tore off two pieces of tape and made a big X with them over his mouth. I then returned to the front of the room. As I glanced at Mark to see how he was doing he winked at me.

"Give thanks to the Lord, call on His name." –Psalm 105:1

That did it! I started laughing. The class cheered as I walked back to Mark's desk, removed the tape and shrugged my shoulders. His first words were, "Thank you for correcting me, Sister!"

At the end of the year I was asked to teach junior-high math. The years flew by, and before I knew it Mark was in my classroom again. He was more handsome than ever and just as polite. Since he had to listen carefully to my instructions in the new math, he did not talk as much in ninth grade as he had in the third.

One Friday, things just didn't feel right. We had worked hard on a new concept all week, and I sensed that the students were frowning, frustrated with themselves – and edgy with one another. I had to stop this crankiness before it got out of hand. So, I asked them to list the names of the other students in the room on two sheets of paper, leaving a space between each name. Then I told them to think of the nicest thing they could say about of each of their classmates and write it down. It took the remainder of the class period to finish the assignment, and as the students left the room each one handed me the papers. Charlie smiled.

That Saturday, I wrote down the name of each student on a sheet of paper, and I listed what everyone else had said about that individual. On Monday, I gave each student his or her list. Before long, the entire class was smiling. "Really?" I heard whispered, "I never knew that meant anything to anyone!" "I didn't know others liked me so much!"

No one ever mentioned those papers in class again. I never knew if they discussed them after class or with their parents, but it didn't matter. The exercise had accomplished its purpose. The students were happy with themselves and one another again.

That group of students moved on. Several years later, after I returned from vacation, my parents met me at the airport. As we were driving home, Mother asked me the usual questions about the trip – the weather, my experiences in general. There was a light lull in the conversation. Mother gave Dad a side-ways glance and simply says, "Dad?" My father cleared his throat as he usually did before something important., "the Eklund's called last night," he began. "Really?" I said. "I haven't heard from them in years. I wonder how Mark is."

Dad responded quietly," Mark was killed in Vietnam", he said." The funeral is tomorrow, and his parents would like it if you could attend." To this day I can still point to the exact spot on I-494 where Dad told me about Mark.

I had never seen a serviceman in a military coffin before. Mark looked so handsome, so mature. All I could think at that moment was, Mark, I would give all the masking tape in the world if only you would talk to me.

"Give thanks to the Lord, call on His name." –Psalm 105:1

The church was packed with Mark's friends. Chuck's sister sang The Battle Hymn of the Republic.

Why did it have to rain on the day of the funeral? It was difficult enough at the graveside. The pastor said the usual prayers, and the bugler played taps. One by one those who loved Mark took a last walk by the coffin and sprinkled it with holy water.

I was the last one to bless the coffin. As I stood there, one of the soldiers who had acted as pallbearer came up to me. "Were you Mark's math teacher?" He asked. I nodded as I continued to stare at the coffin. "Mark talked about you a lot." he said.

After the funeral, most of Mark's former class mates headed to Chuck's farmhouse for lunch. Mark's mother and father were there, obviously waiting for me. "We want to show you something," his father said, taking a wallet out of his pocket. "They found this on Mark when he was killed. We thought you might recognize it."

Opening the billfold, he carefully removed two worn pieces of notebook paper that had obviously been taped, folded and refolded many times. I knew without looking that the papers were the ones on which I had listed all the good things each of Mark's classmates had said about him. "Thank you so much for doing that" Mark's mother said. "As you can see, Mark treasured it."

Mark's classmates started to gather around us. Charlie smiled rather sheepishly and said, "I still have my list. It's in the top drawer my desk at home." Chuck's wife said, "Chuck asked me to put this in our wedding album." "I have mine too." Marilyn said. "It's in my diary." Then Vicki, another classmate, reached into her pocketbook, took out her wallet and showed her worn and frazzled list to the group. "I carry this with me at all times." Vicki said without batting an eyelash. "I think we all saved our lists."

That's when I finally sat down and cried. I cried for Mark and for all his friends who would never see him again.

Sister Helen Mrosla
Franciscan Nun

Three Volunteers

A preacher concluded that his church was getting into serious financial troubles.

While checking the church storeroom, he discovered several big cartons of new bibles that had never been opened and distributed.

"Give thanks to the Lord, call on His name." –Psalm 105:1

So at his Sunday sermon, he asked for three volunteers from the congregation who would be willing to sell the bibles door-to-door for $10 each to raise the desperately needed money for the church.

Jack, Paul and Louie all raised their hands to volunteer for the task. The minister knew that Jack and Paul earned their living as salesmen and were likely capable of selling some bibles. But he had serious doubts about Louie who was a local farmer, who had always kept to himself because he was embarrassed by his speech impediment.

Poor Louie stuttered badly. But, not wanting to discourage Louis, the minister decided to let him try anyway.
He sent the three of them away with the back seat of their cars stacked with bibles.

He asked them to meet with him and report the results of their door-to-door selling efforts the following Sunday.

Eager to find out just how successful they were, the minister immediately asked Jack, "Well, Jack, how did you make out selling our bibles last week"

Proudly handing the reverend an envelope, Jack replied, "Using my sales prowess, I was able to sell bibles, and here's the $100 I collected on behalf of the church."

"Fine job, Jack!" The minister said, vigorously shaking his hand. "You're indeed a fine salesman and the Church is indebted to you."

Turning to Paul, "And Paul, how many bibles did you sell for the church last week"

Paul, smiling and sticking out his chest, confidently replied," I am a professional salesman. I sold 28 bibles on behalf of the church, and here's $280 I collected."

The minister responded, "That's absolutely splendid, Paul. You are truly a professional salesman and the church is also indebted to you."

Apprehensively, the minister turned to Louie and said, "And Louie, did you manage to sell any bibles last week?" Louie silently offered the minister a large envelope.

The minister opened it and counted the contents. "What is this?" the minister exclaimed. "Louie, there's $3000 in here! Are you suggesting that you sold 300 bibles for the church, door to door, in just one week?"

"Give thanks to the Lord, call on His name." –Psalm 105:1

Louie just nodded! That's impossible!" both Jack and Paul said in unison. "We are professional salesmen, yet you claim to have sold 10 times as many bibles as we could."

"Yes, this does seem unlikely." the minister agreed. "I think you'd better explain how you managed to accomplish this, Louie."

Louie shrugged. "I-I-I re-re-really do-do-don't kn-kn-know f-f-f-for sh-sh-sh-sure," he stammered.

Impatiently, Paul interrupted. "For crying out loud, Louie, just tell us what you said to them when they answered the door!"

"A-a-all I-I-I s-s-said wa-wa-was," Louie replied , "W-w-w-would y-y-y-you I-I-I-I-I-like t-t-to b-b-b-buy th-th-th-this b-b-b-b-bible f-f-for t-t-ten b-b-b-bucks -o-o-o-or-wo-wo-would yo-you j-j-j-just I-I-like m-m-me t-t-to st-st-stand h-h-here and r-r-r-r-read it t-to y-y-you"

A Christmas Dinner Story
Distributed by email – December 30, 1999

This is a first-person account from a mother about her family as they ate dinner on Christmas Day in a small restaurant many miles from their home.

Nancy, the mother, relates, we were the only family with children in the restaurant. I sat Erick in a high chair and noticed everyone was quietly eating and talking.

Suddenly, Erik squealed with glee and said, "Hi there." He pounded his fat baby hands on the highchair tray. His eyes were wide with excitement and his mouth was bared in a toothless grin, He wriggled and giggled with merriment.

"Give thanks to the Lord, call on His name." –Psalm 105:1

I looked around and saw the source of this merriment. It was a man with a tattered rag of a coat; dirty, greasy and worn. His pants were baggy with a zipper at half-mast and his toes poked out of would-be shoes. His shirt was dirty and his hair was uncombed and unwashed. His whiskers were too short to be called a beard and his nose was so varicose it looked like a road map.

We were too far from him to smell, but I was sure he smelled. His hands waved and flapped on loose wrists. "Hi there, baby; hi there, big boy. See ya, buster," the man said to Erik. My husband and I exchanged looks, "What do we do?"

Erik continued to laugh and answer, "Hi, hi there." Everyone in the restaurant noticed and looked at us and then at the man. The old geezer was creating a nuisance with my beautiful baby.

Our meal came and the man began shouting from across the room, "Do ya know patty cake? Do you know peek-a-boo? Hey, look, he knows peek-a-boo." Nobody thought the old man was cute. He was obviously drunk. My husband and I were embarrassed. We ate in silence; all except for Erik, who was running though his repertoire for the admiring skid-row bum, who in turn, reciprocated with his cute comments.

We finally got through the meal and headed for the door. My husband went to pay the check and told me to meet him in the parking lot. The old man sat poised between me and the door, "Lord, just let me out of here before he speaks to me or Erik," I prayed.

As I drew closer to the man, I turned my back trying to sidestep him and avoid any air he might be breathing. As I did, Erik leaned over my arm, reaching with both arms in a baby's pick-me-up, position. Before I could stop him, Erik had propelled himself from my arms to the man's arms.

Suddenly a very old smelly man and a very young baby consummated their love relationship. Erik in an act of total trust, love and submission laid his tiny head upon the man's ragged shoulder. The man's eyes closed and I saw tears hover beneath his lashes. His aged hands full of grime, pain, and hard labor –gently, so gently cradled my baby's bottom and stroked his back.

No two beings have ever loved so deeply for so short a time. I stood awestruck. The old man rocked and cradled Erik in his arms for a moment, and then his eyes opened and set squarely on mine. He said in a firm commanding voice, "You take care of this baby."

Somehow, I managed, "I will" from a throat that contained a stone.

"Give thanks to the Lord, call on His name." –Psalm 105:1

He pried Erik from his chest unwillingly, longingly, as though he were in pain. I received my baby, and the man said, "God bless you, ma'am, you've given me my Christmas gift."

I said nothing more than a muttered thanks. With Erik in my arms, I ran for the car. My husband was wondering why I was crying and holding Erik so tightly, and why I was saying, "My God, my God, forgive me,"

I had just witnessed Christ's love shown through the innocence of a tiny child who saw no sin, who made no judgement; a child who saw a soul, and a mother who saw a suit of clothes.

I was a Christian who was blind, holding a child who was not, I felt it was God asking— "Are you willing to share your son for a moment?" When He shared His Son for all eternity.

That ragged old man, unwittingly, had reminded me, "To enter the Kingdom of God, we must become as little children."

The Sandpiper
Received in an email

By Mary Sherman

She was six years old when I first met her on the beach near where I live. I drive to this beach, a distance of three or four miles, whenever the world begins to close in on me.

She was building a sand castle or something and looked up, her eyes as blue as the sea. "Hello," she said. I answered with a nod, not really in the mood to bother with a small child.

"I'm building," she said. 'I see that. What is it? I asked, not really caring.

"Oh, I don't know, I just like the feel of sand."

That sounds good, I thought, and slipped off my shoes. A Sandpiper glided by.

"That's a joy," the child said.

"It's a what?"

"It's a joy. My mama says Sandpipers come to bring us joy."

"Give thanks to the Lord, call on His name." –Psalm 105:1

The bird went gliding down the beach. Good-bye joy, I muttered to myself, hello pain, and turned to walk on. I was depressed; my life seemed completely out of balance.

"What's your name?", she wouldn't give up.

"Mary," I answered. "I'm Mary Sherman."

"Mine's Wendy... I'm six."

"'Hi, Wendy."

She giggled. "You're funny." she said.

In spite of my gloom, I laughed too and walked on. Her musical giggle followed me. "Come again, Mrs. S," she called. "We'll have another happy day."

The next few days consisted of a group of unruly Boy Scouts, PTA meetings and an ailing mother. The sun was shining one morning as I took my hands out of the dishwater. I need a Sandpiper, I said to myself, gathering up my coat.

The ever-changing balm of the seashore awaited me. The breeze was chilly but I strode along, trying to recapture the serenity I needed.

"Hello, Mrs. S" she said. "Do you want to play?"

"What did you have in mind? I asked, with a twinge of annoyance.

"I don't know. You say."

"How about charades?"' I asked sarcastically. The tinkling laughter burst forth again.

"I don't know what that is," she replied

"Then let's just walk," I said.

Looking at her, I noticed the delicate fairness of her face. "Where do you live?" I asked.

"Over there." She pointed toward a row of summer cottages.

Strange, I thought, in winter. "Where do you go to school?"

"I don't go to school. Mommy says we're on vacation."

"Give thanks to the Lord, call on His name." –Psalm 105:1

She chattered little girl talk as we strolled up the beach, but my mind was on other things. When I left for home, Wendy said it had been a happy day. Feeling surprisingly better, I smiled at her and agreed.

Three weeks later, I rushed to my beach in a state of near panic. I was in no mood to even greet Wendy. I thought I saw her mother on the porch and felt like demanding she keep her child at home.

"Look, if you don't mind," I said crossly when Wendy caught up with me, "I'd rather be alone today." She seemed unusually pale and out of breath.

"Why?" she asked.

I turned to her and shouted, "Because my mother died!" and thought, My God, why was I saying this to a little child

"'Oh," she said quietly, "then this is a bad day."

"Yes," I said, "and yesterday and the day before and -- oh, go away!"

"Did it hurt?" she inquired.

"Did what hurt?" I was exasperated with her, with myself.

"When she died?"

"Of course it hurt!" I snapped, misunderstanding, wrapped up in myself. I strode off.

A month or so after that, when I next went to the beach, she wasn't there. Feeling guilty, ashamed, and admitting to myself I missed her, I went up to the cottage after my walk and knocked at the door. A drawn looking young woman with honey-colored hair opened the door.

"Hello,' I said, "I'm Mary Sherman. I missed your little girl today and wondered where she was."

"Oh yes, Mrs. Sherman, please come in. Wendy spoke of you so much I'm afraid I allowed her to bother you. If she was a nuisance, please, accept my apologies."
"Not at all -- she's a delightful child." I said, suddenly realizing that I meant what I had just said.

"Wendy died last week, Mrs. Sherman. She had leukemia. Maybe she didn't tell you."

Struck dumb, I groped for a chair. I had to catch my breath.

"Give thanks to the Lord, call on His name." –Psalm 105:1

'She loved this beach, so when she asked to come, we couldn't say no. She seemed so much better here and had a lot of what she called happy days. But the last few weeks, she declined rapidly..." Her voice faltered, "She left something for you, if only I can find it. Could you wait a moment while I look?"

I nodded stupidly, my mind racing for something to say to this lovely young woman. She handed me a smeared envelope with 'MRS. S' printed in bold childish letters. Inside was a drawing in bright crayon hues -- a yellow beach, a blue sea, and a brown bird. Underneath was carefully printed: *A SANDPIPER TO BRING YOU JOY.*

Tears welled up in my eyes, and a heart that had almost forgotten to love opened wide. I took Wendy's mother in my arms. "I'm so sorry, I'm so sorry, I'm so sorry," I uttered over and over, and we wept together. The precious little picture is framed now and hangs in my study. Six words -- one for each year of her life -- that speak to me of harmony, courage, and undemanding love.

A gift from a child with sea blue eyes and hair the color of sand - who taught me the gift of love.

Editor's Note:

Although this story is written in the first person, the author was not the person who allegedly had the encounter with the child, and is merely repeating a story she heard years earlier.

The One Christmas Carol that has always baffled me.
Distributed by email - Author unknown

What in the world do leaping lords, French hens, swimming swans, and especially the partridge who won't come out of the pear tree have to do with Christmas?

Today, I found out. From 1558 until 1829, Roman Catholics in England were not permitted to practice their faith openly. Someone during that era wrote this carol as a catechism song for young Catholics.

It has two levels of meaning: the surface meaning plus a hidden meaning known only to members of their church. Each element in the carol has a code word for a religious reality, which the children could remember.

The partridge in a pear tree was Jesus Christ.

"Give thanks to the Lord, call on His name." –Psalm 105:1

8

Two turtle doves were the Old and New Testaments.

Three French hens stood for faith, hope and love.

The four calling birds were the four gospels of Matthew, Mark, Luke & John.

The five golden rings recalled the Torah or Law, the first five books of the Old Testament.

The six geese a-laying stood for the six days of creation.

Seven swans a-swimming represented the sevenfold gifts of the Holy Spirit: Prophesy, Serving, Teaching, Exhortation, Contribution, Leadership, and Mercy.

The eight maids a-milking were the eight beatitudes.

Nine ladies dancing were the nine fruits of the Holy Spirit: Love, Joy, Peace, Patience, Kindness, Goodness, Faithfulness, Gentleness, and Self Control.

The ten lords a-leaping were the Ten Commandments.
The eleven pipers piping stood for the eleven faithful disciples.

The twelve drummers drumming symbolized the twelve points of belief in The Apostles' Creed.

So, there is your history for today. This knowledge was shared with me and I found it interesting and enlightening and now I know how that strange song became a Christmas Carol...so pass it on if you wish.

"He tends his flock like a shepherd: He gathers the lambs in his arms and carries them close to his heart;" **Isaiah 40:11**

"Give thanks to the Lord, call on His name." –Psalm 105:1

A Beautiful Christmas Story
Distributed by email – December, 2007

Pa never had much compassion for the lazy or those who squandered their means and then never had enough for the necessities. But for those who were genuinely in need, his heart was as big as all outdoors. It was from him that I learned the greatest joy in life comes from giving, not from receiving.

It was Christmas Eve 1881. I was fifteen years old and feeling like the world had caved in on me because there just hadn't been enough money to buy me the rifle that I'd wanted so badly that year for Christmas. We did the chores early that night for some reason. I just figured Pa wanted a little extra time so we could read in the Bible. So, after supper was over I took my boots off and stretched out in front of the fireplace and waited for Pa to get down the old Bible. I was still feeling sorry for myself and, to be honest, I wasn't in much of a mood to read scripture. But Pa didn't get the Bible; instead he bundled up and went outside.

I couldn't figure it out because we had already done all the chores. I didn't worry about it long though. I was too busy wallowing in self-pity. Soon Pa came back in. It was a cold clear night out and there was ice in his beard. "Come on, Matt," he said. "Bundle up good, it's cold out tonight." I was really upset then.
Not only wasn't I getting the rifle for Christmas, now Pa was dragging me out in the cold, and for no earthly reason that I could see. We'd already done all the chores, and I couldn't think of anything else that needed doing, especially on a night like this. But I knew Pa was not very patient at one dragging one's feet when he'd told them to do something, so I got up and put my boots back on and got my cap, coat, and mittens. Ma gave me a mysterious smile as I opened the door to leave the house. Something was up, but I didn't know what. Outside, I became even more dismayed. There in front of the house was the work team, already hitched to the big sled.

Whatever it was we were going to do wasn't going to be a short, a quick, little job. I could tell. We never hitched up the big sled unless we were going to haul a big load. Pa was already up on the seat, reins in hand. I reluctantly climbed up beside him. The cold was already biting at me. I wasn't happy. When I was on, Pa pulled the sled around the house and stopped in front of the woodshed. He got off and I followed. "I think we'll put the high sideboards on" he said, but whatever it was we were going to do would be a lot bigger with the high sideboards on.

When we had exchanged the sideboards, Pa went into the woodshed and came out with an armload of wood-the wood I'd spent all summer hauling down from the mountain, and then all fall sawing into blocks and splitting. What was he doing? Finally, I said something. "Pa" I asked," what are you doing?" You been by the Widow Jensen's lately?" he asked.

"Give thanks to the Lord, call on His name." –Psalm 105:1

The Widow Jensen lived about two miles down the road. Her husband had died a year or so before and left her with three children, the oldest being eight. Sure, I'd been by, but so what? "Yeah," I said, "why?" "I rode by just today," Pa said. "Little Jakey was out digging around in the woodpile trying to find a few chips. They're out of wood, Matt." That was all he said and then he turned and went back into the woodshed for another armload of wood. I followed him. We loaded the sled so high that I began to wonder if the horses would be able to pull it. Finally, Pa called a halt to our loading, then we went to the smokehouse and Pa took down a big ham and a side of bacon. He handed them to me and told me to put them in the sled and wait. When he returned he was carrying a sack of flour over his right shoulder and a smaller sack of something in his left hand." What's in the little sack?" I asked. "Shoes. They're out of shoes. Little Jakey just had gunnysacks wrapped around his feet when he was out in the woodpile this morning. I got the children a little candy too. It just wouldn't be Christmas without a little candy."

We rode the two miles to Widow Jensen's pretty much in silence. I tried to think through what Pa was doing. We didn't have much by worldly standards. Of course, we did have a big woodpile, though most of what was left now was still in the form of logs that I would have to saw into blocks and split before we could use it. We also had meat and flour, so we could spare that, but I knew we didn't' have any money, so why was PA buying shoes and candy?
Really, why was he doing any of this? Widow Jensen had closer neighbors than us. It shouldn't have been our concern.

We came in from the blind side of the Jensen house and unloaded the wood as quietly as possible, and then we took the meat and flour and shoes to the door. We knocked. The door opened a crack and a timid voice said, "Who is it?" "Lucas Miles, Ma'am and my son, Matt. Could we come in a bit?" Widow Jensen opened the door and let us in. She had a blanket wrapped around her shoulders. The children were wrapped in another and all were sitting in front of the fireplace by a very small fire that hardly gave off any heat at all. Widow Jensen fumbled with a match and finally lit the lamp. "We brought you a few things, Mrs. Jensen," Pa said and set down the sack of flour. I put the meat on the table. Then Pa handed her the sack that had shoes, taking them out one pair at a time. There was a pair for her and one for each of the children—sturdy shoes, the best, shoes that would last. I watched her carefully. She bit her lower lip to keep it from trembling and the tears filled her eyes and started running down her cheeks. She looked up at Pa like she wanted to say something, but it wouldn't come out. "We brought a load of wood too, Ma'am," Pa said, then he turned me and said," Matt, go and bring enough in to last for a while. Let's get the fire up to size and heat this place up.

I wasn't the same person when I went back out to bring in the wood. I had a big lump in my throat and, much as I hate to admit it, there were tears in my eyes too. In my mind, I kept seeing those three kids huddled around the fireplace and

"Give thanks to the Lord, call on His name." –Psalm 105:1

their mother standing there with tears running down her cheeks and so much gratitude in her heart that she couldn't speak.

My heart swelled within me and a joy filled my soul that I'd never known before. I had given at Christmas many times before, but never when it had made so much difference. I could see we were literally saving the lives of these people. I soon had the fire blazing and everyone's spirts soared. The kids started giggling when Pa handed each a piece of candy and Widow Jensen looked on with a smile that probably hadn't crossed her face for a long time. She finally turned to us, "God Bless you," she said. "I know the Lord Himself has sent you. The children and I have been praying that he would send one of his angels to us."

In spite of myself, the lump returned to my throat and the tears welled up in my eyes again. I'd never thought of Pa in those exact terms before, but after Widow Jensen mentioned it I could see that it was probably true. I was sure that a better man than Pa had never walked the earth. I started remembering all the times he had gone out of his way for Ma and me, and many others. The list seemed endless as I thought on it. Pa insisted that everyone try on the shoes before we left. I was amazed when they all fit and I wondered how he had known what sizes to get. Then I guessed that if he was on an errand for the Lord that the Lord would make sure he got the right sizes. Tears were running down Widow Jensen's face again when we stood up to leave.

Pa took each of the kids in his big arms and gave them a hug. They clung to him and didn't want us to go. I could see that they missed their pa, and I was glad that I still had mine. At the door Pa turned to Widow Jensen and said, "The Mrs. wanted me to invite you and the children over for Christmas dinner tomorrow. The turkey will be more than the three of us can eat, and a man can get cantankerous if he has to eat turkey for too many meals. We'll be by to get you and the kids about eleven. Twill be nice to have some little ones around again. Matt, here hasn't been little for quite a spell."

I was the youngest. My two older brothers and two older sisters were all married and had moved away. Widow Jensen nodded and said, "Thank you, Brother Miles. I don't have to say, "May the Lord bless you,' I know for certain that He will."

Out on the sled I felt a warmth that came from deep within and I didn't even notice the cold. When we had gone a ways, Pa turned to me and said, "Matt, I want you to know one thing. Your Ma and me have been tucking a little money away here and there all year so we could buy that rifle for you, but we didn't have quite enough.

Then yesterday a man who owed me a little money from years back came by to make things square. Your ma and me were real excited, thinking that now we could get you that rifle, and I started in to town this morning to do just that. But on

"Give thanks to the Lord, call on His name." –Psalm 105:1

the way, I saw little Jakey out scratching in the woodpile with his feet wrapped in those gunnysacks and I knew what I had to do.

So, son, I spent the money for the shoes and a little candy for those children. I hope you understand." I understood, and my eyes became wet with tears again. I understood very well, and I was so glad Pa had done it.

Just then the rifle seemed very low on my list of priorities, Pa had given me a lot more. He had given me the look on Widow Jensen's face and the radiant smiles of her three children for the rest of my life. Whenever I saw any of the Jensen's, I felt the same joy I felt riding home beside Pa that night.

Pa had given me much more than a rifle that night, he had given me the best Christmas of my life.

The Birth of the Song "Precious Lord"

Reverend Thomas A. Dorsey 1899-1993

"Back in 1932, I was 32 years old and a fairly new husband. My wife, Nettie and I were living in a little apartment on Chicago's Southside.

One hot August afternoon I had to go to St. Louis, where I was to be the featured soloist at a large revival meeting. I didn't want to go. Nettie was in the last month of pregnancy with our first child. But a lot of people were expecting me in St. Louis......

"Give thanks to the Lord, call on His name." –Psalm 105:1

kissed Nettie good-bye, clattered downstairs to our Model A and, in a fresh Lake Michigan breeze, chugged out of Chicago on Route 66. However, outside the city, I discovered that in my anxiety at leaving, I had forgotten my music case. I wheeled around and headed back.

I found Nettie sleeping peacefully. I hesitated by her bed; something was strongly telling me to stay. But eager to get on my way, and not wanting to disturb Nettie, I shrugged off the feeling and quietly slipped out of the room with my music.

The next night, in the steaming St. Louis heat, the crowd called on me to sing again and again. When I finally sat down, a messenger boy ran up with a Western Union telegram. I ripped open the envelope. Pasted on the yellow sheet were the words: YOUR WIFE JUST DIED....

When I got back, I learned that Nettie had given birth to a boy. I swung between grief and joy. Yet that night, the baby died. I buried Nettie and our little boy together, in the same casket. Then I fell apart. For days, I closeted myself. I felt that God had done me an injustice. I didn't want to serve Him anymore or write gospel songs. I just wanted to go back to that jazz world I once knew so well.

But then, as I hunched alone in that dark apartment those first sad days, I thought back to the afternoon I went to St. Louis. Something kept telling me to stay with Nettie. Was that something God Oh, if I had paid more attention to Him that day, I would have stayed and been with Nettie when she died.

From that moment on I vowed to listen more closely to Him. But still I was lost in grief. Everyone was kind to me, especially a friend, Professor Fry, who seemed to know what I needed.

On the following Saturday evening, he took me up to Malone's Poro College, a neighborhood music school. It was quiet; the late evening sun crept through the curtained windows.

I sat down at the piano, and my hands began to browse over the keys. Something happened to me then. I felt at peace. I felt as though I could reach out and touch God. I found myself playing a melody, once into my head they just seemed to fall into place:

Precious Lord, take my hand, lead me on, let me stand I am tired, I am weak, I am worn, through the storm, through the night lead me on to the light, take my hand, precious Lord, Lead me home.

The Lord gave me these words and melody, He also healed my spirit.

"Give thanks to the Lord, call on His name." –Psalm 105:1

I learned that when we are in our deepest grief, when we feel farthest from God, this is when He is closest, and when we are most open to His restoring power. And so, I go on living for God willingly and joyfully, until that day comes when He will take me and gently lead me home."

Reverend Thomas A. Dorsey
1899-1993

Christmas at the Gas Station
Distributed by email - Author unknown

The old man sat behind the counter of his gas station on a cold Christmas Eve. Business had been brisk with people gassing up their vehicles to visit relatives. He hadn't been anywhere in years since his wife had passed away. It was just another day to him. He didn't hate Christmas, just couldn't find a reason to celebrate.

He was sitting there looking at the snow that had been falling for the last hour, wondering why he was still around, when the door opened and a man who looked homeless stepped through.

Instead of throwing the man out, "Old George" as he was known by his customers, told the man to come and sit by the heater and warm up.

"Thank you, that's very kind. I don't want to be a bother," said the stranger. "It's pretty cold out there... but maybe I should just go."

"Not without somethin' hot in your belly." George said.

"Give thanks to the Lord, call on His name." –Psalm 105:1

He turned, opening a wide mouth Thermos and handed it to the stranger. "It ain't much, but it's hot and tasty. Stew... made it myself. When you're done, there's coffee, and it's fresh."

Just at that moment he heard the "ding" of the driveway bell. "Excuse me, be right back," George said.

There in the driveway was an old '53 Chevy. Steam was rolling out of the front.

The driver was panicked. "Meester, help!" said the driver. In halting English with a thick Spanish accent, he continued. "Mi esposa... she have the baby. Mi car, she broken."

George peered under the hood. There was so much steam that he couldn't see much of anything. His guess, though, was that the block had cracked from the cold. The car was as dead as a doornail. "You ain't going nowhere in this thing," George said as he turned away.

"Por favor, meester -- Ayudame! You can help me?" Tears stood in his frantic eyes. The door of the office closed behind George as he stepped inside. He went to the office wall, got the keys to his old truck, and went back outside. He walked around the building, opened the garage, started the truck and drove it around to where the couple was waiting.

"Here, take my truck," he said. "She ain't the best thing to look at, but she runs real good. You can bring her back after the baby comes. I'll see what I can do about your car." George helped put the woman in the truck, and watched as it sped off into the night.

He turned and walked back inside the gas station. "Glad I gave 'em the truck; their tires were shot, too. Not safe." George thought he was talking to the stranger, but the man had left. The Thermos was on the desk, empty, with a used coffee cup beside it.

"Well, at least he got something in his belly," George thought.

George went back outside to see if the old Chevy would start. It cranked slowly, but finally caught.

"Give thanks to the Lord, call on His name." –Psalm 105:1

He pulled it into the garage where the truck had been, thinking he'd tinker with it later on. When business dropped off around dinnertime, he discovered that the block hadn't cracked, it was just the bottom hose on the radiator. "Well, shoot, I can fix this," he said to himself. So, he put a new one on.

"Those tires ain't gonna get 'em through the winter, though." The snow treads on his wife's old Lincoln were the same size. They were like new, and he wasn't going to drive that car anyway. So, he put them on the couple's Chevy.

As he was working, he heard what sounded like gunshots. He ran outside.

Across the street next to a squad car, he found a middle-aged policeman lying on the ground. Blood was coming from his right shoulder. The officer was moaning, "Please... help..."

The officer's shoulder radio wasn't functioning. Following the cop's instructions, George tried to raise someone via the police car's communication system, only to find that a bullet had left it useless.

George remembered the training he had received in the Army as a medic. He knew the wound needed pressure to stop the bleeding. The uniform company had been there that morning and had left a bag of clean shop towels. He wadded up a bunch of them and used duct tape to bind the wound. "Hey, they say duct tape can fix anythin'," he said, trying to make the policeman feel at ease.

Running back to the garage, he tried to call 911, only to find that his phone had no dial tone. Now what? Blankets and something for pain, George thought. All he had was the Arthritis-Strength Tylenol he used for his back. He went back to find the officer sitting up.

"These oughta help with the hurtin'." He wrapped up the policeman and handed him the pills along with a bottle of water.

"You hang in there, I'm gonna try to find somethin' to get you off this cold street." A few minutes later, he returned with a large 4-way dolly, and managed to haul the policeman over to the warmth of his shop.

"Thanks," said the officer. "You probably should have just left me there. The guy that shot me is still in the area."

George sat down beside him, "I would never leave an injured man in the Army, and I sure wasn't gonna leave you." George pulled back the bandage to check for bleeding. "Looked worse than what it was, I think. Bullet passed right through ya. Seems to have missed the important stuff, though. I think with time yer gonna be right as rain."

"Give thanks to the Lord, call on His name." –Psalm 105:1

George got up and poured a cup of coffee. "How ya take it?" he asked. "None for me," said the officer.

"Oh, ya gotta try this! Best coffee in the city. Too bad I ain't got no donuts to go with it." The officer laughed and winced at the same time.

George was about to head off to try to find a working phone when the front door of the shop flew open. In burst, a young man with a gun.

"Give me all your cash! Do it now!" the young man yelled. His hand was shaking and George could tell that he had never done anything like this before.

"That's the guy that shot me!" exclaimed the officer.

"Son, why are you doing this?" asked George, "You need to put that cannon away. Somebody else might get hurt."

The young man acted confused. "Shut up, old man, or I'll shoot you, too. Now give me your cash!"

The cop was reaching for his service revolver. "Put that dang thing away," George said to the cop, "we got one too many in here already."

He turned his attention to the young man. "Son, it's Christmas Eve. If you need money that bad, well then... here. It ain't much, only $150 bucks, but it's all I got. Just put that pea shooter away."

George pulled the pile of bills out of the cash register, and handed it to the young man, reaching for the barrel of the gun at the same time. The young man released his grip on the gun, fell to his knees and began to cry.

"I'm not very good at this am I? All I wanted was to get something for my wife and son," he went on. "I lost my job, and our rent is due. The landlord said he was going to evict us if we didn't come up with at least part of the money we owe him. My car got repossessed last week. I've already sold every last thing I own that's worth a plugged nickel..."

George handed the gun to the cop. "Son, we all get in a bit of squeeze now and then. The road gets hard sometimes, but we make it through the best we can." He got the young man to his feet, and sat him down on a chair across from the officer.

"Sometimes we do stupid things." George handed the boy a cup of coffee. "Bein' stupid is one of the things that makes us human. Comin' in here with a gun ain't the answer. Now sit there and get warm, and we'll sort this thing out."

"Give thanks to the Lord, call on His name." –Psalm 105:1

The young man had stopped crying. He looked over at the cop. "Sorry I shot you," he said sheepishly. "I was so scared when you came up behind me that it just kinda went off.

"Shut up and drink your coffee." the cop said.

George could hear the sounds of sirens outside. A police car and an ambulance skidded to a halt. Two cops threw open the door, guns drawn. "Chuck! You ok?" one of the cops asked the wounded officer.

"Not bad for a guy who took a bullet. How'd you find me?"

"GPS locator in the car. Best thing since sliced bread. Somebody called 911, reporting shots fired over this way. When you didn't answer the dispatcher, she put two and two together.

Who did this?" the other cop asked, looking suspiciously at the young man.

Chuck answered him, "I don't know. The guy ran off into the dark. Just dropped his weapon and ran." He handed over the now wiped-clean pistol to his fellow patrolman. George and the young man exchanged puzzled looks.

"This guy work here?" the wounded cop asked, eyeing his shooter.

"Yep," George said after only a brief hesitation. "Just hired him today. Boy lost his job last week."

The paramedics came in and loaded Chuck onto the stretcher. The young man leaned over the wounded cop before he was wheeled away, and whispered, "Why?"

Chuck just said, "Merry Christmas, kid... You, too, George! And thanks for everything."

"Well, looks like you got one doozie of a break there. That oughta solve some of your problems."

While the young man sat with his head in his hands, George went into the back room, and came out with a small box, which he handed to the boy. "Here ya go, son... something for the little woman.

I don't think Martha would mind. She said it would come in handy some day."

The young man looked inside to see a good-sized diamond pendant. "I can't take this," said the young man. "It's gotta mean something to you."

"Give thanks to the Lord, call on His name." –Psalm 105:1

'You're right... and now it'll mean somethin' to you," replied George. "I got my memories of Martha. That's all I need."

From under the counter, George pulled out another box holding a car and a tanker truck.

They were toys that the oil company had left for him to sell. "Here's a present for that son of yours."

The young man began to cry again as he handed back the $150 that the old man had handed him earlier.

"And what are you supposed to buy Christmas dinner with -- or pay that rent? You keep that, too," George said. "Now git on home to your family before you git yerself into more hot water!"

The young man turned with tears streaming down his face. "I'll be here in the morning for work, if you really meant that job offer."

"Sorry. That won't work. I'm closed on Christmas Day," George said. "See ya the day after."

George watched the boy head off down the street. He turned to lock up the garage, thinking, "Whew, what a day! Nobody would believe it." When he entered the shop, he was surprised to see that the homeless man had returned.

"Hey! Where'd you come from? I thought you left?"

"Give thanks to the Lord, call on His name." –Psalm 105:1

"Oh, I've been here all along. In fact, I've always been here," said the stranger, to the old man's confusion. "You say you don't celebrate Christmas. Why is that?"

"Well, after my wife passed away, I just couldn't see what the big to-do was all about. Trimmin' a tree seemed like a waste of a good pine tree. Bakin' cookies like I used to with Martha just wasn't the same by myself, and besides I was gettin' a little chubby."

The stranger put his hand on the garage owner's shoulder. "But you DO celebrate the Christmas holiday, George. You gave me food and drink and warmed me when I was cold and hungry. The woman with child will bear a son, and he will become a great doctor.

The policeman you helped will go on to save 19 people from being killed by terrorists. The young man who tried to rob you will make you a rich man and not take any of the fortune for himself. That is the spirit of the season, and you keep it as well as any man."

George was taken aback by all this stranger had said. "And how do you know all this?" asked the old man.

"Trust me, my friend, I have the inside track on this sort of thing. And when your days are done, have no fear. You will be with Martha again." The stranger moved toward the door. "If you will excuse me, George... I have to go home now. There's a big celebration planned."

George watched as the old denim jacket and the torn jeans that the stranger was wearing faded into a white robe. The room was suddenly bathed in a golden light.

"You see, George... it's my birthday. Merry Christmas!"

George fell to his knees and replied, "Happy Birthday, Lord!"

57 cents

A sobbing little girl stood near a small church from which she had been turned away because it "was too crowded." "I can't go to Sunday School, "she sobbed to the pastor as he walked by.

Seeing her shabby, unkempt appearance, the pastor guessed the reason and, taking her by the hand, took her inside and found a place for her in the Sunday school class. The child was so happy that they found room for her, that she went to bed that night thinking of the children who have no place to worship Jesus.

"Give thanks to the Lord, call on His name." –Psalm 105:1

Some two years later, this child lay dead in one of the poor tenement buildings and the parents called for the kindhearted pastor, who had befriended their daughter, to handle the final arrangements.

As her poor little body was being moved, a worn and crumpled purse was found which seemed to have been rummaged from some trash dump. Inside was found 57 cents and a note scribbled in childish handwriting which read, "This is to help build the little church bigger so more children can go to Sunday School. For two years she had saved for this offering of love.

When the pastor tearfully read that note, he knew instantly what he would do. Carrying this note and the cracked, red pocketbook to the pulpit, he told the story of her unselfish love and devotion. He challenged his deacons to get busy and raise enough money for the larger building. But the story does not end there! A newspaper learned of the story and published it. It was read by a Realtor who offered them a parcel of land worth many thousands. When told that the church could not pay so much, he offered it for 57 cents.

Church members made large donations. Checks came from far and wide. Within five years the little girl's gift had increased to $250,000.00--a huge sum for that time (near the turn of the century). Her unselfish love had paid a large dividend.

When you are in the city of Philadelphia, look up Temple Baptist Church, with a seating capacity of 3,300 and Temple University, where hundreds of students are trained annually.

Temple Baptist Church

Have a look, too, at the Good Samaritan Hospital and at a Sunday School building which houses hundreds of Sunday Schoolers, so that no child in the area will ever need to be left outside during Sunday school time.

In one of the rooms of this building may be seen the picture of the sweet face of the little girl whose 57 cents, so sacrificially saved, made such remarkable history. Alongside of it is a portrait of the kind pastor, Dr. Russel H. Conwell, author of the book, "Acres of Diamonds"

An interesting story, which goes to show WHAT GOD CAN DO WITH 57 CENTS.

See http://www.snopes.com/glurge/57cents.asp

"Give thanks to the Lord, call on His name." –Psalm 105:1

"It is no Secret"

Back in the 50's there was a well-known radio Host/comedian/song writer in Hollywood named Stuart Hamblen who was noted for his drinking, womanizing, partying, etc.

One of his bigger hits at the time was **"I won't go hunting with you Jake, But I'll go chasing women"**

One day, along came a young preacher holding a tent revival. Hamblen had him on his radio show presumably to poke fun at him.

In order to gather more material for his show, Hamblen showed up at one of the revival meetings.

Early in the service the preacher announced, "There is one man in this audience who is a big fake." There were probably others who thought the same thing, But Hamblen was convinced that he was the one the preacher was talking about (some would call that conviction) But he was having none of that.

Still the words continued to haunt him until a couple of nights later he showed up drunk at the preacher's hotel door around 2 AM demanding that the preacher pray for him!

But the preacher refused, saying, "This is between you and God and I'm not going to get in the middle of it."

But he did invite Stuart in and they talked until about 5 AM at which point Stuart dropped to his knees and with tears, cried out to God.

But that is not the end of the story. Stuart quit drinking, quit chasing women, quit everything that was 'fun.' Soon he began to lose favor with the Hollywood crowd.

He was ultimately fired by the radio station when he refused to accept a beer company as a sponsor.

Hard times were upon him. He tried writing a couple of "Christian" songs but the only one that had much success was "This Old House", written for his friend Rosemary Clooney.

"Give thanks to the Lord, call on His name." –Psalm 105:1

As he continued to struggle, a longtime friend named John took him aside and told him, "All your troubles started when you 'got religion,' Was it worth it all?" Stuart answered simply, "Yes."

Then his friend asked, "You liked your booze so much, don't you ever miss it?" And his answer was, "No." John then said, "I don't understand how you could give it up so easily."

And Stuart's response was, "It's no big secret. All things are possible with God." To this John said, "That's a catchy phrase. You should write a song about it." And as they say, "The rest is history."

The song Carl Stuart Hamblen wrote was **"It Is No Secret."** "It is no secret what God can do. What He's done for others, He'll do for you. With arms wide open, He'll welcome you. It is no secret; what God can do...."

By the way... The friend was John Wayne. And the young preacher who refused to pray for Stuart Hamblen?..............that was Billy Graham

I have a Praise

The pastor asked if anyone in the congregation would like to express praise for answered prayers.

Suzie Smith stood and walked to the podium. She said, "I have a praise. Two months ago, my husband, Phil, had a terrible bicycle wreck and his scrotum was completely crushed. The pain was excruciating and the doctors didn't know if they could help him."

"Give thanks to the Lord, call on His name." –Psalm 105:1

You could hear a muffled gasp from the men in the congregation as they imagined the pain that poor Phil must have experienced.

"Phil was unable to hold me or the children," she went on, "and every move caused him terrible pain. We prayed as the doctors performed a delicate operation, and it turned out they were able to piece together the crushed remnants of Phil's scrotum and wrap wire around it to hold it in place."

Again, the men in the congregation cringed and squirmed uncomfortably as they imagined the horrible surgery performed on Phil.

"Now," she announced in a quivering voice, "thank the Lord, Phil is out of the hospital and the doctors say that with time his scrotum should recover completely."

All the men sighed with unified relief. The pastor rose and tentatively asked if anyone else had something to say.

A man stood up and walked slowly to the podium. He said, "I'm Phil."

The entire congregation held its breath. "I just want to tell my wife the word is sternum."

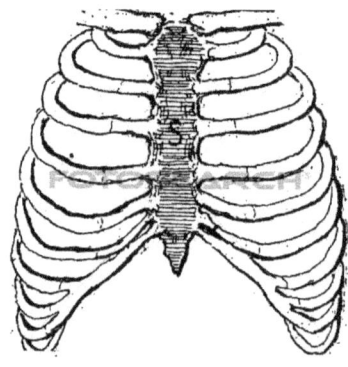

"Give thanks to the Lord, call on His name." –Psalm 105:1

Viewed from Heaven...

Yard Work – As viewed from Heaven

(overheard in a conversation between God and St. Francis)

God: Francis, you know all about gardens and nature; what in the World is going on down there in the U.S.? What happened to the Dandelions, violets, thistles and the stuff I started eons ago?

I had a perfect no-maintenance garden plan. Those plants grow in any type of soil, withstand drought, and multiply with abandon. The nectar from the long-lasting blossoms attracts butterflies, honeybees, and flocks of songbirds. I expected to see a vast garden of color by now. All I see are patches of green.

St. Francis: It's the tribes that settled there, Lord. They are called the Suburbanites. They started calling your flowers "weeds" And went to great lengths to kill them and replace them with grass.

God: Grass? But it is so boring, it's not colorful. It doesn't attract butterflies, bees or birds, only grubs and sod worms. It's temperamental with temperatures. Do these Suburbanites really want grass growing there?

St. Francis: Apparently not, Lord. As soon as it has grown a little, they cut it.... sometimes two times a week.

God: They cut it? Do they bale it like hay?

St. Francis: Not exactly, Lord. Most of them rake it up and put it in bags.

God: They bag it? Why? Is it a cash crop? Do they sell it?

St. Francis: No sir, just the opposite. They pay to throw it away.

God: Now let me get this straight...they fertilize it to make it grow and when it does grow, they cut it off and pay to throw it away?

St. Francis: Yes, sir.

God: These Suburbanites must be relieved in the summer when we cut back on the rain and turn up the heat. That surely slows the growth and saves them a lot of work.

"Give thanks to the Lord, call on His name." –Psalm 105:1

St. Francis: You aren't going to believe this Lord, but when the grass stops growing so fast, they drag out hoses and pay more money to water it so they can continue to mow it and pay to get rid of it.

God: What nonsense! At least they kept some of the trees. That was a sheer stroke of genius, if I do say so myself. The trees grow leaves in the spring to provide beauty and shade in the summer. In the autumn, they fall to the ground and form a natural blanket to keep the moisture in the soil and protect the trees and bushes. Plus, as they rot, the leaves become compost to enhance the soil. It's a natural circle of life.

St. Francis: You'd better sit down, Lord. As soon as the leaves fall, the Suburbanites rake them into great piles and pay to have them hauled away.

God: No way! What do they do to protect the shrubs and tree roots in the winter to keep the soil moist and loose?

St Francis: After throwing the leaves away, they go out and buy something called mulch. They haul it home and spread it around in place of the leaves.

God: And where do they get this mulch?

St. Francis: They cut down the trees and grind them up to make mulch.

God: Enough! I don't want to think about this anymore. Saint Catherine, you're in charge of the arts. What movie have you scheduled for us tonight?

St. Catherine: "Dumb and Dumber," Lord. It's a really stupid movie about...

God: Never mind -I think I just heard the whole story from Saint Francis!

"Give thanks to the Lord, call on His name." –Psalm 105:1

Watch

Watch your thoughts; they become words.

Watch your words; they become actions.

Watch your actions; they become habits.

Watch your habits; they become character.

Watch your character; it becomes your destiny.

Does anyone know who this is?

There was an atheist couple who had a child. The couple never told their daughter anything about the Lord.

One night when the little girl was five years old, the parents fought with each other and the dad shot the mom right in front of the child.
Then the dad shot himself. The little girl watched it all.

She then was sent to a foster home. The foster mother was a Christian and took the child to church.

On the first day of Sunday School, the foster mother told the teacher that the girl had never heard of Jesus, and to have patience with her. The teacher held up a picture of Jesus and said, "Does anyone know who this is?"

The little girl said, "I do, that's the man who was holding me the night my parents died."

Email from John Buckman
December 30, 1999

Editor's Note:

This piece (of unknown origin) about an orphaned girl who sees a picture of Jesus in Sunday school and identifies him as the man who comforted her the night her father killed her mother and himself is a fairly typical example of glurge, ordinarily unremarkable save for one facet: it has been turned into a smash hit by Nashville songwriter Harley Allen and country singer John Michael Montgomery. The song, titled "The Little Girl," was penned by Allen after his brother forwarded him the above-quoted glurge via e-mail. "It moved me more than I'd been moved in years by a story," Allen said. "I grabbed the guitar and just started writing. It didn't take any time at all, about 10 to 15 minutes."

"Give thanks to the Lord, call on His name." –Psalm 105:1

Quizzical Questions

What do they call pastors in Germany?
German Shepherds

Who was the greatest financier in the Bible?
Noah. He was floating his stock while everyone else was in liquidation.

Who was the greatest female financier in the Bible?
Pharaoh's daughter. She went down to the bank of the Nile and drew out a little prophet.

Who was the greatest comedian in the Bible?
Samson. He brought the house down.

What excuse did Adam give to his children as to why he longer lives in Eden?
Your mother ate us out of house and home.

What kind of motor vehicles are in the Bible?
Jehovah drove Adam and Eve out of the Garden in a Fury. David's Triumph was heard throughout the land. Also, probably a Honda, because the apostles were all in one Accord.

Which servant of God was the most flagrant lawbreaker in the Bible?
Moses. He broke all 10 commandments all at once.

Which area of Palestine was especially wealthy?
The area around Jordan, the banks were always overflowing.

Who is the greater babysitter mentioned in the Bible?
David. He rocked Goliath to a very deep sleep.

Which Bible character had no parents?
Joshua, son of Nun.

Why didn't they play cards on the Ark?
Because Noah was standing on the deck.

Did you know it's a sin for a woman to make coffee?
Yup, it's in the Bible. It says........." He-brews"

Remember when the funniest jokes were the clean ones?
They still are! A cheerful heart is good medicine...

"Give thanks to the Lord, call on His name." –Psalm 105:1

Church Billboard Signs...

"God will answer your prayer, if you will wait and listen."
Helton Springs (TN) Missionary Baptist Church
Rutledge, Tennessee

"Adam & Eve, the first people to not read the Apple Terms & Conditions."
St. Mark's Anglican Church

"Too hot to keep changing sign. Sin – Bad! Jesus - Good! Details inside."
Holy Trinity Roman Catholic Church

"Whoever stole our AC units, keep one. It is hot where you're going."
Clays Mill Road Baptist Church

"Be the kind of person your pet thinks you are."
Wesley Chapel United Methodist Church

"Honk if you love Jesus. Text while driving if you want to meet him."
Stonebridge Church of God, Ozark, Al

"Just love everyone, I'll sort 'em out later. -God"
Walnut Grove Baptist Church

"Catch up with JESUS. Lettuce Praise & Relish Him. "Cuz He loves me from my head to-ma-toes."

Unknown

"Forgive your enemies – it messes with their heads."
Central Baptist Church

"Give thanks to the Lord, call on His name." –Psalm 105:1

"Jesus is watching, but the police have radar."　　　　Unknown

"Give God what's right, not what's left." Fellowship Baptist Church

"Read the Bible – it will scare the hell out of you." Wyldwood Baptist Church

"Dust on your Bible could lead to dirt in your life." Crossroads Church of Christ

"God does not believe in Atheists; therefore, Atheists do not Exist."
　　　　　　　　　　Palm Heights Baptist Church

"Forbidden fruits create many jams."
　　　　　　　　　　First Church of God

"You have one new friend request from Jesus. CONFIRM__ IGNORE___"
　　　　　　　　　　St. Gibbs Presbyterian Church

"Get off of Facebook and into my book –God" Fall Creek Baptist Church

"Free Coffee, Everlasting Life. Yes, membership has its privileges."
　　　　　　　　　　Goodwood United Church

"Get Right or Get Left." Community Worship Center Church of God

"Prayer –wireless access to God with no roaming fee."
First United Pentecostal Church of Ragley

"Why pay for GPS? Jesus gives direction for free." United New Church of Christ.

"Jesus, your get out of Hell Free Card." Crossroads of Faith Church

"Give thanks to the Lord, call on His name." –Psalm 105:1

'Life is a puzzle. Look here for the missing peace." Guess Road Baptist Church

"Sign Broke – Message inside." Corinth Baptist Church

"Son screen prevents sin burn." Beacon Baptist Ministries

"Try Jesus" If you don't like Him, the Devil will take you back." Western Hills Church of Christ

"Easter is more than something to dye for." Kelham Baptist Church

"God wants spiritual fruits, not religious nuts". United New Church of Christs.

"There are some questions that can't be answered by Google". Claude Presbyterian Church

"If you would shut up, you could hear God's voice." Valliant Church of God

"Need a lifeguard? Ours walks on water." Dayspring Community Church

"Be an organ donor, give your heart to Jesus."   Church of the living Water.

"Give thanks to the Lord, call on His name." –Psalm 105:1

Jokes that can be told in Church…

An elderly woman died last month. Having never married, she requested no male pallbearers. In her handwritten instructions for her memorial service, she wrote, "They wouldn't take me out while I was alive, I don't want them to take me out when I'm dead."

Squirrels in Church

The **Presbyterian church** called a meeting to decide what to do about their squirrels. After much prayer and consideration, they concluded the squirrels were predestined to be there and they shouldn't interfere with God's divine will.

At the **Baptist church,** the squirrels had taken an interest in the baptistery. The deacons met and decided to put a water slide on the baptistery and let the squirrels drown themselves. The squirrels liked the slide and, unfortunately, knew instinctively how to swim so twice as many squirrels showed up the following week.

The **Methodist church** decided that they were not in a position to harm any of God's creatures. So, they humanely trapped their squirrels and set them free near the Baptist Church. Two weeks later the squirrels were back when the Baptists took down the water slide.

But the **Catholic Church** came up with a very creative strategy. They baptized all the squirrels and consecrated them as members of the church. Now they only see them on Christmas and Easter.

Not much was heard from the **Jewish synagogue**; they took the first squirrel and circumcised him. They haven't seen a squirrel since.

"Give thanks to the Lord, call on His name." –Psalm 105:1

Bubba

Bubba goes to the revival and listens to the preacher. After awhile, the preacher asks anyone with needs to come forward and be prayed over.

Bubba gets in line and when it's his turn the preacher says, "Bubba, what do you want me to pray about" Bubba says, "Preacher, I need you to pray for my hearing."

So the preacher puts one finger in Bubba's ear and the other hand on top of his head and prays a while. After a few minutes, he removes his hands and says, "Bubba how's your hearing now?"

Bubba says, "I don't know preacher, it's not until next Wednesday."

Smart Cop

A police recruit was asked during the exam, "What would you do if you had to arrest your own mother" He answered," Call for backup."

The Chauffeur!

Evangelist Billy Graham was returning to Charlotte after a speaking engagement and when his plane arrived there was a limousine there to transport him to his home. As he prepared to get into the limo, he stopped and spoke to the driver.

'You know' he said, 'I am 87 years old and I have never driven a limousine. Would you mind if I drove it for a while?'

The driver said, 'No problem. Have at it.'

Billy gets into the driver's seat and they head off down the highway. A short distance away sat a rookie State Trooper operating his first speed trap. The long black limo went by him doing 70 in a 55-mph zone. The trooper pulled out and easily caught the limo and he got out of his patrol car to begin the procedure.

The young trooper walked up to the driver's door and when the glass was rolled down, he was surprised to see who was driving. He immediately excused himself and went back to his car and called his supervisor.

He told the supervisor, 'I know we are supposed to enforce the law... But I also know that important people are given certain courtesies. I need to know what I should do because I have stopped a very important person.'

"Give thanks to the Lord, call on His name." –Psalm 105:1

The supervisor asked, 'Is it the governor?' The young trooper said, 'No, he's more important than that.'

The supervisor said, 'Oh, so it's the president.' The young trooper said, 'No, he's even more important than that.'

The supervisor finally asked, 'Well then, who is it?' The young trooper said, 'I think it's Jesus.

"What makes you think that?" Asked his supervisor, Because, he's got Billy Graham for a chauffeur!

God and I are tight

An 80-year-old man went for a physical. All of his tests come back with normal results. The doctor said, "George, everything looks great. How are you doing mentally and emotionally Are you at peace with God"

George replied, "God and I are tight. He knows I have poor eyesight, so he's fixed it so when I get up in the middle of the night to go to the bathroom, poof! The light goes on. When I'm done, poof! The light goes off."

"Wow, that's incredible," the doctor said. A little later in the day, the doctor called George's wife. "Ethel," he said, "George is doing fine! But I had to call you because I'm in awe of his relationship with God. Is it true that when he gets up during the night to go to the bathroom that, poof! The light goes on in the bathroom, and when he's done, poof! The light goes off"

"Oh, my Lord!" Ethel exclaimed, "He's peeing in the refrigerator again!"

Support A Family

The prospective father-in-law asked, "Young man, can you support a family?" The surprised groom-to-be replied, "Well, no, I was just planning to support your daughter. The rest of you will have to fend for yourselves."

"Give thanks to the Lord, call on His name." –Psalm 105:1

Oh No!

Some drunk staggers into a Catholic Church, enters a confessional booth, sits down, but says nothing.

The Priest coughs a few times to get his attention but the drunk continues to sit there.

Finally, the Priest pounds three times on the wall. The drunk mumbles, "ain't no use knockin', there's no toilet paper on this side either!"

Life After Death

"Do you believe in life after death?" the boss asked one of his employees.

"Yes Sir," the new employee replied.

"Well, then, that makes everything just fine," the boss went on. "After you left early yesterday to go to your grandmother's funeral, she stopped in to see you!"

Father (This One Is Priceless!)

A little boy got on the bus, sat next to a man reading a book, and noticed he had his collar on backwards.

The little boy asked why he wore his collar backwards.

The man, who was a priest, said, 'I am a Father.'

The little boy replied, 'My Daddy doesn't wear his collar like that.'

The priest looked up from his book and answered, "I am the Father of many.'

The boy said, "My Dad has 4 boys, 4 girls and two grandchildren and he doesn't wear his collar that way!'

The priest, getting impatient, said. 'I am the Father of hundreds', and went back to reading his book.

The little boy sat quietly thinking for a while, then leaned over and said,

"Maybe you should wear a condom, and put your pants on backwards instead of your collar."

"Give thanks to the Lord, call on His name." –Psalm 105:1

Easter Dress

At the beginning of a children's sermon, one girl came up to the alter wearing a beautiful dress. As the children were sitting down around the pastor, he leaned over and said to the girl, "That is a very pretty dress. Is it your Easter dress?" The girl replied almost directly into the pastor's clip-on mike, "Yes, and my mom says it's a bitch to iron."

God's Problem Now

The graveside service just barely finished, when there was massive clap of thunder, followed by a tremendous bolt of lightning, accompanied by even more thunder rumbling in the distance.

The little old man looked at the pastor and calmly said, 'Well, she's there.'

Church Gossip

Mildred the church gossip and self-appointed monitor of the church's morals, kept sticking her nose into other people's business. Several members did not approve of her activities, but feared her enough to maintain their silence.

She made a mistake, however, when she accused Frank, a new member, of being an alcoholic after she saw his old pickup parked in front of the town's only bar one afternoon.

She emphatically told Frank (and several others) that everyone seeing it there would know what he was doing!

Frank, a man of few words, stared at her for a moment and just turned and walked away.

He didn't explain, defend, or deny. He said nothing.

Later that evening, Frank quietly parked his pickup in front of Mildred's house .... walked home .... and left it there all night.

You don't stop laughing because you grow old. You grow old because you stop laughing!

"Give thanks to the Lord, call on His name." –Psalm 105:1

The High Octane, Holy Bed Pan

A young Nun who worked for a local home health care agency was out making her rounds when she ran out of gas. As luck would have it, there was a gas station just one block away. She walked to the station to borrow a can with enough gas to start the car and drive to the station for a fill up.

The attendant regretfully told her that the only gas can he owned had just been loaned out, but if she would care to wait he was sure it would be back shortly.

Since the Nun was on the way to see a patient, she decided not to wait and walked back to her car. After looking through her car for something to carry to the station to fill with gas, she spotted a bedpan she was taking to the patient.

Always resourceful, she carried it to the station, filled it with gasoline, and carried it back to her car. As she was pouring the gas into the tank of her car, two men watched her from across the street.

One of them turned to the other and said: "I know that it is said that Jesus turned water into wine, but if that car starts, I'll go to church every Sunday for the rest of my life."

A FLORIDA COURT SETS ATHEIST HOLY DAY

In Florida, an atheist created a case against Easter and Passover Holy days. He hired an attorney to bring a discrimination case against Christians and Jews and observances of their holy days. The argument was that it was unfair that atheists had no such recognized days.

The case was brought before a judge. After listening to the passionate presentation by the lawyer, the judge banged his gavel declaring, "Case dismissed!"

The lawyer immediately stood and objecting to the ruling saying, "Your honor, how can you possibly dismiss this case?

The Christians have Christmas, Easter and others. The Jews have Passover, Yom Kippur and Hanukkah, yet my client and all other atheists have no such holidays."

"Give thanks to the Lord, call on His name." –Psalm 105:1

The judge leaned forward in his chair saying, "But you do. Your client, counselor, is woefully ignorant." The lawyer said," Your Honor, we are unaware of any special observance or holiday for atheists."

The judge said, "The calendar says April 1st is April Fool's Day.

Psalm 14:1 states, 'The fool says in his heart, there is no God.'

Thus, it is the opinion of this court, that, if your client says there is no God, then he is a fool. Therefore, April 1st is his day!!!

Court is adjourned!"

You gotta love a Judge who knows his Scripture!

Email from Charles Shupienus
August 23, 2017

"Give thanks to the Lord, call on His name." –Psalm 105:1

In God We Trust

On the outskirts of a small town, there was a big, old pecan tree just inside the cemetery fence. One day, two boys filled up a bucketful of nuts and sat down by the tree, out of sight, and began dividing the nuts. "One for you, one for me, one for you, one for me," said one boy. Several dropped and rolled down toward the fence.

Another boy came riding along the road on his bicycle. As he passed, he thought he heard voices from inside the cemetery. He slowed down to investigate. Sure enough, he heard, "One for you, one for me, one for you, one for me ...."

He just knew what it was. He jumped back on his bike and rode off. Just around the bend he met an old man with a cane, hobbling along.

"Come here quick," said the boy, "you won't believe what I heard! Satan and the Lord are down at the cemetery dividing up the souls!"

The man said, "Beat it kid, can't you see it's hard for me to walk." When the boy insisted though, the man hobbled slowly to the cemetery. Standing by the fence they heard, "One for you, one for me. One for you, one for me."

The old man whispered, "Boy, you've been tellin' me the truth. Let's see if we can see the Lord..." Shaking with fear, they peered through the fence, yet were still unable to see anything.

The old man and the boy gripped the wrought iron bars of the fence tighter and tighter as they tried to get a glimpse of the Lord.

At last they heard, "One for you, one for me. That's all. Now let's go get those nuts by the fence and we'll be done...."

They say the old man had the lead for a good half-mile before the kid on the bike passed him.

Email from Jim Atkinson
September 29, 2017

"Give thanks to the Lord, call on His name." –Psalm 105:1

Tailgating Woman

An honest man was being tailgated by a stressed-out woman on a busy boulevard. Suddenly, the light turned yellow, just in front of him.

He did the right thing, stopping at the crosswalk, even though he could have beaten the red light by accelerating through the intersection.

The tailgating woman hit the roof, and the horn, screaming in frustration as she missed her chance to get through the intersection.

As she was still in mid-rant, she heard a tap on her window and looked up into the face of a very serious police officer. The officer ordered her to exit her car with her hands up. He took her to the police station where she was searched, finger printed, photographed and placed in a holding cell.

After a couple of hours, a policeman approached the cell and opened the door. She was escorted back to the booking desk where the arresting officer was waiting with her personal effects.

He said, "I'm very sorry for this mistake. You see, I pulled up behind your car while you were blowing your horn, flipping off the guy in front of you, and cussing a blue streak at him.

"I noticed the 'Choose Life' license plate holder, the ' What Would Jesus Do' bumper sticker, the 'Follow Me to Sunday-School' bumper sticker, and the chrome-plated Christian fish emblem on the trunk.

Naturally, I assumed you had stolen the car."

Just What Would Jesus Do?
Just The Right Thing !

"Give thanks to the Lord, call on His name." –Psalm 105:1

Satan Appeared

People were in their pews talking at church. Suddenly, Satan appeared at the front of the church. Everyone started screaming and running for the front entrance, trampling each other in a frantic effort to get away from evil incarnate.

Soon everyone had exited the church except for one elderly gentleman who sat calmly in his pew without moving, seeming oblivious to the fact that God's ultimate enemy was in his presence.

Satan walked up to the old man and said, "Don't you know who I am?"

The man replied, "Yep, sure do." "Aren't you afraid of me?" Satan asked.

"Nope, sure ain't." said the man.

"Don't you realize I can kill you with a word?" asked Satan.

"Don't doubt it for a minute," returned the old man, in an even tone.

"Did you know that I could cause you profound horrifying, AGONY for all eternity?"

"Yep." was the calm reply.

"And you're still not afraid?" asked Satan.

"Nope." said the old man.

More than a little perturbed, Satan asked, "Well, why aren't you afraid of me?"

The man calmly replied, "Been married to your sister for 48 years."

"Give thanks to the Lord, call on His name." –Psalm 105:1

Church bulletin Bloopers...

Thank God for church ladies with typewriters. These sentences actually appeared in church bulletins or were announced in church service

Bertha Belch, a missionary from Africa, will be speaking tonight at Calvary Methodist. Come hear   Bertha Belch all the way from Africa.

The Fasting and Prayer Conference includes meals.

The sermon this morning: "Jesus Walks on the Water." The sermon tonight: "Searching for Jesus."

Our youth basketball team is back in action Wednesday at 8 PM in the recreation hall. Come out and watch us kill Christ the King.

Ladies, don't forget the rummage sale. It's a chance to get rid of those things not worth keeping around the house. Don't forget to bring your husbands.

The peacemaking meeting scheduled for today has been canceled due to a conflict.

Remember in prayer the many who are sick of our community.

Smile at someone who is hard to love.

Say "Hello" to someone who doesn't care much about you.

"Give thanks to the Lord, call on His name." –Psalm 105:1

Don't let worry kill you off......let the Church help.

Miss Charlene Mason sang "I will not pass this way again," giving obvious pleasure to the congregation.

For those of you who have children and don't know it, we have a nursery downstairs.

Next Thursday there will be tryouts for the choir. They need all the help they can get.

Barbara remains in the hospital and needs blood donors for more transfusions. She is also having trouble sleeping. She has requested tapes of Pastor Gary's sermons.

The Rector will preach his farewell message after which the choir will sing, "Break Forth into Joy."

Irving Benson and Jessie Carter were married on October 24 in the church and so ends a friendship that began in their school days.

A bean supper will be held on Tuesday evening in the church hall. Music will follow.

At the evening service tonight, the sermon topic will be "What Is Hell". Come early and listen to our choir practice.

Eight new choir robes are currently needed due to the addition of several new members and to the deterioration of some older ones.

"Give thanks to the Lord, call on His name." –Psalm 105:1

Scouts are saving aluminum cans, bottles and other items to be recycled. Proceeds will be used to cripple children.

Please place your donation in the envelope along with the deceased person you want remembered.

Attend and you will hear an excellent speaker and heave a healthy lunch.

The church will host an evening of fine dining, super entertainment and gracious hostility.

Pot-luck supper Sunday at 5:00 PM - prayer and medication to follow.

The ladies of the Church have cast-off clothing of every kind. They may be seen in the basement on Friday afternoon.

This evening at 7 PM there will be a hymn singing in the park across from the Church. Bring a blanket and come prepared to sin.

Ladies Bible Study will be held Thursday morning at 10 AM. All ladies are invited to lunch in the Fellowship Hall after the B. S. is done.

The pastor would appreciate it if the ladies of the congregation would lend him their electric girdles for the pancake breakfast next Sunday.

Low Self Esteem Support Group will meet Thursday at 7 PM. Please use the back door.

"Give thanks to the Lord, call on His name." –Psalm 105:1

The eighth-graders will be presenting Shakespeare's Hamlet in the Church basement Friday at 7 PM. The congregation is invited to attend this tragedy.

Weight Watchers will meet at 7 PM at the First Presbyterian Church. Please use large double door at the side entrance.

Next Sunday a special collection will be taken to defray the cost of the new carpet. All those wishing to do something on the new carpet will come forward and do so.

The rosebud on the alter this morning is to announce the birth of David Alan Balzer, the sin of REV. and Mrs. Julius Belzer.

The service will close with "Little Drops of Water." One of the ladies will start quietly and the rest of the congregation will join in.

This afternoon there will be a meeting in the South and North ends of the church. Children will be baptized at both ends.

This being Easter Sunday, we will ask Mrs. Lewis to come forward and lay an egg on the alter.

Thursday at 5:00 pm there will be an ice cream social. All ladies giving milk will please come early.

Wednesday, the ladies Liturgy Society will meet. Mrs. Jones will sing, "Put Me in My Little Bed" accompanied by the pastor.

The Associate Minister unveiled the church's new tithing campaign slogan last Sunday: "I Upped My Pledge - Up Yours."

"Give thanks to the Lord, call on His name." –Psalm 105:1

Preachers and Deacons...

Sermons We See

By Edgar A. Guest

I'd rather see a sermon than hear one any day,

I'd rather one should walk with me than merely show the way,

The eye's a better pupil and more willing than the ear;

Fine counsel is confusing, but example's always clear;

And the best of all the preachers are the men who live their creeds,

For to see the good in action is what everybody needs.

I can soon learn how to do it if you'll let me see it done,

I can watch your hands in action, but your tongue too fast may run.

And the lectures you deliver may be very wise and true;

But I'd rather get my lesson by observing what you do.

For I may misunderstand you and the high advice you give,

But there's no misunderstanding how you act and how you live.

As read by Don Stanfill
First Baptist Church
Church Hill, Tennessee
October 15, 2017

"Give thanks to the Lord, call on His name." –Psalm 105:1

Country Funeral

Distributed by email - Author unknown

As a young minister, I was asked by a funeral director to hold a graveside service in a new cemetery for a derelict man (with no family or friends) who had died while traveling through the area.

The cemetery was way back in the country. This man would be the first to be laid to rest at this new cemetery.

As I was not familiar with the backwoods area, I became lost.

Being the typical man, I didn't stop for directions. And when I finally arrived an hour late, I saw a crew and a backhoe, but the hearse was nowhere in sight.

The workmen were eating lunch. I apologized for my tardiness, but the workers just looked puzzled. I stepped to the side of the open grave, to find the vault lid already in place.

I assured the workers I would not hold them long, but this was the proper thing to do.

As the workers gathered around, still eating their lunch. I poured out my heart and soul.

As I preached, the workers began to say "Amen," "Praise the Lord" and "Glory," (they must have all been Baptist).

I preached, and I preached, like I'd never preached before. I began from Genesis and worked all the way through to Revelation. I preached for 45 minutes.

It was a long service. Finally, I closed in prayer and it was finished.

As I was walking to my car, I felt that I had done my duty and I would leave with a renewed sense of purpose and dedication, in spite of my tardiness.

As I was opening the door and taking off my coat, I overheard one of the workers saying to another.......

"Ya know, I've been putting in septic tanks for 20 years, but I ain't never seen anything like that before."

"Give thanks to the Lord, call on His name." –Psalm 105:1

New Preacher

Late on a Sunday evening a wife, sat down and told her Husband she was completely exhausted.

He said," What have you got to be so tired about? I just finished three days of sermons and two special ones, So I'm the one who is so tired"

She said," Yes Dear, but remember I had to listen to all of them."

Pastor's Business Card

A new pastor was visiting in the homes of his parishioners.

At one house, it seemed obvious that someone was at home, but no answer came to his repeated knocks at the door. Therefore, he took out a card and wrote "Revelation 3:20" on the back of it and stuck it in the door.

When the offering was processed the following Sunday, he found that his card had been returned. Added to it was this cryptic message, "Genesis 3:10."

Reaching for his Bible to check out the citation, he broke up in gales of laughter. Revelation 3:20 begins "Behold, I stand at the door and knock."

Genesis 3:10 reads, "I heard your voice in the garden and I was afraid for I was naked."

New Preacher Visitation

The new pastor in a small Southern town was making his rounds meeting the members of his flock. The widow Parker happy to see the new pastor invited him in for a cup of tea. While waiting for Mrs. Parker to make the tea the pastor noticed a bowl of peanuts on the coffee table next to the piano. He ate one then he ate a second one. Man, those peanuts tasted so good he had some more. He ate all of the peanuts.

As Ms., Parker was pouring the tea the embarrassed pastor apologized for eating all of the peanuts. Ms. Parker replied, "aw shucks pastor, ain't no problem, I can't eat them, all I do is suck the chocolate off of them.

"Give thanks to the Lord, call on His name." –Psalm 105:1

Unanswered Prayer

The preacher's 5-year-old daughter noticed that her father always paused and bowed his head for a moment before starting his sermon. One day, she asked him why.

'Well, Honey,' he began, proud that his daughter was so observant of his messages. 'I'm asking the Lord to help me preach a good sermon.'

'How come He doesn't answer it?' she asked.

The Pastor and his son

A good reminder of God's Love.

Every Sunday afternoon, after the morning service at the church, the Pastor and his eleven-year-old son would go out into their town and hand out Gospel Tracts.

This particular Sunday afternoon, as it came time for the Pastor and his son to go to the streets with their tracts, it was very cold outside, as well as pouring down rain. The boy bundled up in his warmest and driest clothes and said, "OK, dad, I'm ready."

His Pastor dad asked, "Ready for what?"

"Dad, it's time we gather our tracts together and go out." Dad responds, "Son, it's very cold outside and it's pouring down rain." The boy gives his dad a surprised look, asking, "But Dad, aren't people still going to Hell, even though it's raining?"

Dad answers, "Son, I am not going out in this weather." Despondently, the boy asks, "Dad, can I go? Please?'

His father hesitated for a moment then said, "Son, you can go. Here are the tracts, be careful son."

"Thanks Dad, and with that, he was off and out into the rain. His eleven-year-old boy walked the streets of the town going door to door and handing everybody he met in the street a Gospel Tract.

After two hours of walking in the rain, he was soaking, bone-chilled wet and down to his VERY LAST TRACT. He stopped on a corner and looked for someone to hand a tract to, but the streets were totally deserted.

"Give thanks to the Lord, call on His name." –Psalm 105:1

Then he turned toward the first home he saw and started up the sidewalk to the front door and rang the doorbell. He rang the bell, but nobody answered. He rang it again and again, but still no one answered. He waited but still no answer.

Finally, this eleven-year-old trooper turned to leave, but something stopped him. Again, he turned to the door and rang the bell and knocked loudly on the door with his fist. He waited, something holding him there on the front porch! He rang again and this time the door slowly opened.

Standing in the doorway was a very sad-looking elderly lady. She softly asked, "What can I do for you, son?" With radiant eyes and a smile that lit up her world, this little boy said, "Ma'am, I'm sorry if I disturbed you, but I just want to tell you that **JESUS REALLY DOES LOVE YOU** and I came to give you my very last Gospel Tract which will tell you all about JESUS and His great LOVE."

With that, he handed her his last tract and turned to leave. She called to him as he departed. "Thank you, son! And God Bless You!"

Well, the following Sunday morning in church Pastor Dad was in the pulpit. As the service began, he asked, "Does anybody have any testimony or want to say anything?"

Slowly, in the back row of the church, an elderly lady stood to her feet. As she began to speak, a look of glorious radiance came from her face, "No one in this church knows me. I've never been here before.

You see, before last Sunday I was not a Christian. My husband passed on some time ago, leaving me totally alone in this world. Last Sunday, being a particularly cold and rainy day, it was even more so in my heart that I came to the end of the line where I no longer had any hope or will to live.

I took a rope and a chair and ascended the stairway into the attic of my home. I fastened the rope securely to a rafter in the roof, then stood on the chair and fastened the other end of the rope around my neck.

Standing on that chair, so lonely and brokenhearted I was about to leap off, when suddenly the loud ringing of my doorbell downstairs startled me.

"Give thanks to the Lord, call on His name." –Psalm 105:1

I thought, 'I'll wait a minute, and whoever it is will go away.' I waited and waited, but the ringing doorbell seemed to get louder and more insistent, and then the person ringing also started knocking loudly. I thought to myself again, 'Who on earth could this be? Nobody ever rings my bell or comes to see me.' I loosened the rope from my neck and started for the front door, all the while the bell rang louder and louder.

When I opened the door, and looked I could hardly believe my eyes, for there on my front porch was the most radiant and angelic little boy I had ever seen in my life. His SMILE, oh, I could never describe it to you!

The words that came from his mouth caused my heart that had long been dead, TO LEAP TO LIFE as he exclaimed with a cherub-like voice, "Ma'am, I just came to tell you that **JESUS REALLY DOES LOVE YOU**." Then he gave me this Gospel Tract that I now hold in my hand.

"As the little angel disappeared back out into the cold and rain, I closed my door and read slowly every word of this Gospel Tract. Then I went up to my attic to get my rope and chair. I wouldn't be needing them anymore.

You see---I am now a Happy Child of the KING. Since the address of your church was on the back of this Gospel Tract, I have come here to personally say THANK YOU to God's little angel who came just in the nick of time and by so doing, spared my soul from an eternity in hell."

There was not a dry eye in the church. And as shouts of praise and honor to THE KING resounded off the very rafters of the building, Pastor Dad descended from the pulpit to the front pew where the little angel was seated.

He took his son in his arms and sobbed uncontrollably. Probably no church has had a more glorious moment, and probably this universe has never seen a Papa that was more filled with love and honor for his son...Except for One.

Our Father also allowed His Son to go out into a cold and dark world. He received His Son back with joy unspeakable, and as all of heaven shouted praises and honor to The King, the Father sat His Beloved Son on a throne far above all principality and power and every name that is named.

"For God so loved the world that he gave his one and only Son, that whoever believes in him shall not perish but have eternal life." **John 3:16**

"Give thanks to the Lord, call on His name." –Psalm 105:1

This Dollar is for you

Little Johnny's Dad gave him a dollar to put in the collection plate during the Sunday service. Johnny was so excited he sat up front in the first pew. Shortly after the Pastor begin to preach, little Johnny began to wave the dollar bill at the preacher.

Unperturbed the pastor continued to preach. After the third time Johnny waved the dollar, the preacher stopped and asked Johnny if he had something he wanted to say about the dollar he kept waiving. Little Johnny said yes sir preacher, this dollar is for you. My Dad said you are the poorest preacher this church has ever had.

92-YEAR-OLD PREACHER

While watching a little TV on Sunday instead of going to church, I watched a Church in Atlanta honoring one of its senior preachers who had been retired many years.

He was 92 at that time and I wondered why the Church even bothered to ask the old gentleman to preach at that age.

After a warm welcome, introduction of this speaker, and as the applause quieted down he rose from his high back chair and walked slowly, with great effort and a sliding gait, to the podium.

Without a note or written paper of any kind he placed both hands on the pulpit to steady himself and then quietly and slowly he began to speak... "When I was asked to come here today and talk to you, your preacher asked me to tell you what was the greatest lesson ever learned in my 50 odd years of preaching.

I thought about it for a few days and boiled it down to just one thing that made the most difference in my life and sustained me through all my trials.

The one thing that I could always rely on when tears and heartbreak and pain and fear and sorrow paralyzed me... the only thing that would comfort me was this verse..........

"Give thanks to the Lord, call on His name." –Psalm 105:1

'Jesus loves me this I know, for the Bible tells me so.
Little ones to Him belong, we are weak but He is strong....
Yes, Jesus loves me... The Bible tells me so.'

When he finished, the church was quiet. You actually could hear his footsteps as he shuffled back to his chair. I don't believe I will ever forget it.

A preacher once stated, "I always noticed that it was the adults who chose the children's hymn 'Jesus Loves Me' (for the children, of course) during a hymn sing, and it was the adults who sang the loudest because I could see they knew it the best."

"Senior version of Jesus Loves Me' Here is a new version just for us who have white hair or no hair at all. For us over middle age (or even those almost there) and all of you others check out this newest version of 'Jesus Loves Me'.

JESUS LOVES ME

Jesus loves me, this I know,
Though my hair is white as snow
Though my sight is growing dim,
Still He bids me trust in Him.

YES, JESUS LOVES ME. YES, JESUS LOVES ME..
YES, JESUS LOVES ME FOR THE BIBLE TELLS ME SO.

Though my steps are oh, so slow,
With my hand in His I'll go
On through life, let come what may,
He'll be there to lead the way. (CHORUS)

When the nights are dark and long,
In my heart He puts a song.
Telling me in words so clear,
'Have no fear, for I am near.' (CHORUS)

When my work on earth is done,
And life's victories have been won.
He will take me home above,
Then I'll understand His love (CHORUS)

I love Jesus, does He know?
Have I ever told Him so?
Jesus loves to hear me say,
That I love Him every day.   (CHORUS)

"Give thanks to the Lord, call on His name." –Psalm 105:1

This suggested next verse has been in my head for years:

> "Jesus is the one I love,
> He was sent from Heaven above;
> gave His life on Calvary;
> paid the price for you and me.

YES, I LOVE JESUS, YES, I LOVE JESUS, YES, I LOVE JESUS, BECAUSE HE FIRST LOVED ME

Ken Henry

Shout and Sing

A relative new and young pastor at a Southern Baptist church in the Smokey Mountains decided he would liven up the Sunday Evening service with a shout and sing singspiration.

He informed the congregation that instead of a sermon tonight, he would shout out a word and the congregation would respond with the hymn that the word reminded them of.

He began with "Cross" and the congregation sang "The Old Rugged Cross. Then came "Jordan" and the congregants responded with "Shall we gather at the River".

The new pastor was pleased with the response and shouted "Jesus" and the congregants sang "Jesus Loves Me.' The last word he shouted was "SEX". Complete silence throughout the congregation and then from the back of the church two widows began to sing "Precious Memories".

Salary Increase

The new minister's wife had a baby. The minister appealed to the congregation for a salary increase to cover the addition to the family. The congregation agreed that it was only fair, and approved it. When the next child arrived, the minister appealed again and the congregation approved again.

Several years and five children later, the congregation was a bit upset over the increasing expense. This turned into a rather loud meeting one night with the minister. Finally, the minster stood and shouted out, "Having children is an Act of God!" An older man in the back stood and shouted back, "Rain and snow are acts of God, too, and we wear rubbers for them!"

"Give thanks to the Lord, call on His name." –Psalm 105:1

The Baptist Dog!

A Baptist preacher and his wife decided to get a new dog.   Ever mindful of the congregation, they knew the dog must also be a Baptist.

They visited kennel after kennel and explained their needs. Finally, they found a kennel whose owner assured them he had just the dog they wanted.

The owner brought the dog to meet the pastor and his wife. "Fetch the Bible," he commanded. The dog bounded to the bookshelf, scrutinized the books, located the Bible, and brought it to the owner. Now find Psalm 23," he commanded. The dog dropped the Bible to the floor, and showing marvelous dexterity with his paws, leafed through and finding the correct passage, pointed to it with his paw. The pastor and his wife were very impressed and purchased the dog. That evening, a group of church members came to visit. The pastor and his wife began to show off the dog, having him locate several Bible verses. The visitors were very impressed.

One man asked, "Can he do regular dog tricks, too" "I haven't tried yet," the pastor replied. He pointed his finger at the dog. "HEEL!" the pastor commanded. The dog immediately jumped on a chair, placed one paw on the pastor's forehead and began to howl.

The pastor looked at his wife in shock and said, "Good Lord! He's "Pentecostal!"

I hate buttermilk

One Sunday morning at a small southern church, the new pastor called on one of his older deacons to lead in the opening prayer.

The deacon stood up, bowed his head and said, "Lord, I hate buttermilk." The pastor opened one eye and wondered where this was going. The deacon continued, "Lord, I hate lard." Now the pastor was totally perplexed. The deacon continued, "Lord, I ain't too crazy about plain flour, but after you mix 'em all together and bake 'em in a hot oven, I just love biscuits".

"Lord help us to realize when life gets hard, when things come up that we don't like, whenever we don't understand what You are doing, that we need to wait and see what You are making. After You get through mixing and baking, it'll probably be something even better than biscuits. Amen"

From Lynn Parker, Sunday School Teacher
First Baptist Church of Church Hill, TN

"Give thanks to the Lord, call on His name." –Psalm 105:1

Practice makes Perfect

A young preacher, who was staying at a clergy-house, was in the habit of retiring to his room for an hour or more each day to practice pulpit oratory. At such times, he filled the house with sounds of fervor and pathos, and emptied of almost everything else. The Bishop chanced to be visiting a friend in this house one day when the budding orator was holding forth.

"Gracious me!" exclaimed the Bishop, starting up in assumed terror, "pray, what might that be?"

"Sit down, Bishop," his friend replied. "that's only young Devon practicing what he preaches."

Leaning Side

Every time I am asked to pray, I think of the old deacon who always prayed, "Lord, prop us up on our leanin' side." After hearing him pray that prayer many times, someone asked him why he prayed that prayer so fervently.

He answered, "Well sir, you see, it's like this.... I got an old barn out back. It's been there a long time, it's withstood a lot of weather, it's gone through a lot of storms, and it's stood for many years. It's still standing, but one day I noticed it was leaning to one side a bit. So, I went and got some pine poles and propped it up on its leaning side so it wouldn't fall.

Then I got to thinking about that and how much I was like that old barn. I been around a long time, I've withstood a lot of life's storms, I've withstood a lot of bad weather in life, I've withstood a lot of hard times, and I'm still standing too. But I find myself leaning to one side from time to time, so I like to ask the Lord to prop us up on our leaning side, 'cause I figure a lot of us get to leaning, at times."

Sometime we get to leaning toward anger, leaning toward bitterness, leaning toward gossip, leaning toward hatred, leaning toward cussing, leaning toward a lot of things that we shouldn't, so we need to pray, "Lord, prop us up on our leaning side," so we will stand straight and tall again, to glorify the Lord.

Author Unknown.

"Give thanks to the Lord, call on His name." –Psalm 105:1

Living Bible

His name is Bill. He has wild hair, wears a T-shirt with holes in it, jeans, and no shoes. This was literally his wardrobe for his entire four years of college. He is brilliant. Kind of profound and very, very bright. He became a Christian while attending college.

Across the street from campus is a well-dressed, very conservative church. They want to develop a ministry to the students but are not sure how to go about it.

One-day Bill decides to go there. He walks in with no shoes, jeans, his T-shirt, and wild hair. The service has already started and so Bill starts down the aisle looking for a seat.

The church is completely packed and he can't find a seat. By now, people are really looking a bit uncomfortable, but no one says anything. Bill gets closer and closer and closer to the pulpit, and when he realizes there are no seats, he just squats down right on the carpet. By now the people are really uptight, and the tension in the air is thick.

About this time, the minister realizes that from way at the back of the church, a deacon is slowly making his way toward Bill.

Now the deacon is in his eighties, has silver-gray hair, and a three-piece suit. A godly man, very elegant, very dignified, very courtly. He walks with a cane and, as he starts walking toward this boy, everyone is saying to themselves that you can't blame him for what he's going to do.

How can you expect a man of his age and of his background to understand some college kid on the floor?

It takes a long time for the man to reach the boy. The church is utterly silent except for the clicking of the man's cane. All eyes are focused on him. You can't even hear anyone breathing. The minister can't even preach the sermon until the deacon does what he has to do.

And now they see this elderly man drop his cane on the floor. With great difficulty, he lowers himself and sits down next to Bill and worships with him so he won't be alone.

Everyone chokes up with emotion. When the minister gains control, he says,

"What I'm about to preach, you will never remember. What you have just seen, you will never forget."

"Give thanks to the Lord, call on His name." –Psalm 105:1

God Lives under the bed

I envy Kevin.

My brother, Kevin, thinks God lives under his bed. At least that's what I heard him say one night.

He was praying out loud in his dark bedroom, and I stopped to listen, "Are you there, God?" he said. "Where are you? Oh, I see. Under the bed...."

I giggled softly and tiptoed off to my own room. Kevin's unique perspectives are often a source of amusement. But that night something else lingered long after the humor. I realized for the first time the very different world Kevin lives in.

He was born 30 years ago, mentally disabled as a result of difficulties during labor. Apart from his size (he's 6-foot-2), there are few ways in which he is an adult.

He reasons and communicates with the capabilities of a 7-year-old, and he always will. He will probably always believe that God lives under his bed, that Santa Claus is the one who fills the space under our tree every Christmas and that airplanes stay up in the sky because angels carry them.

I remember wondering if Kevin realizes he is different. Is he ever dissatisfied with his monotonous life?

Up before dawn each day, off to work at a workshop for the disabled, home to walk our cocker spaniel, return to eat his favorite macaroni-and-cheese for dinner, and later to bed.

The only variation in the entire scheme is laundry, when he hovers excitedly over the washing machine like a mother with her newborn child. He does not seem dissatisfied. He lopes out to the bus every morning at 7:05, eager for a day of simple work.

He wrings his hands excitedly while the water boils on the stove before dinner, and he stays up late twice a week to gather our dirty laundry for his next day's laundry chores.

And Saturdays - oh, the bliss of Saturdays! That's the day my Dad takes Kevin to the airport to have a soft drink, watch the planes land, and speculate loudly on the destination of each passenger inside. "That one's goin' to Chi-car-go!" Kevin shouts as he claps his hands. His anticipation is so great he can hardly sleep on Friday nights. And so goes his world of daily rituals and weekend field trips.

"Give thanks to the Lord, call on His name." –Psalm 105:1

He doesn't know what it means to be discontent. His life is simple. He will never know the entanglements of wealth or power, and he does not care what brand of clothing he wears or what kind of food he eats. His needs have always been met, and he never worries that one day they may not be.

His hands are diligent. Kevin is never so happy as when he is working. When he unloads the dishwasher or vacuums the carpet, his heart is completely in it. He does not shrink from a job when it is begun, and he does not leave a job until it is finished. But when his tasks are done, Kevin knows how to relax.

He is not obsessed with his work or the work of others. His heart is pure.

He still believes everyone tells the truth, promises must be kept, and when you are wrong, you apologize instead of argue.

Free from pride and unconcerned with appearances, Kevin is not afraid to cry when he is hurt, angry or sorry. He is always transparent, always sincere. And he trusts God. Not confined by intellectual reasoning, when he comes to Christ, he comes as a child. Kevin seems to know God - to really be friends with Him in a way that is difficult for an "educated" person to grasp. God seems like his closest companion.

In my moments of doubt and frustrations with my Christianity, I envy the security Kevin has in his simple faith. It is then that I am most willing to admit that he has some divine knowledge that rises above my mortal questions. It is then I realize that perhaps he is not the one with the handicap. I am. My obligations, my fear, my pride, my circumstances - they all become disabilities when I do not trust them to God's care.

Who knows if Kevin comprehends things I can never learn? After all, he has spent his whole life in that kind of innocence, praying after dark and soaking up the goodness and love of God.

 And one day, when the mysteries of heaven are opened, and we are all amazed at how close God really is to our hearts, I'll realize that God heard the simple prayers of a boy who believed that God lived under his bed.

Kevin won't be surprised at all!

Friends are Angels who lift us to our feet when our wings have trouble remembering how to fly!

"Give thanks to the Lord, call on His name." –Psalm 105:1

Family & Friends...

"Many people walk in and out of your life, but only true friends will leave footprints in your heart." – Eleanor Roosevelt

My father often said "the only thing more important in life than your family and your health, is having good friends. In order to have good friends you need to be a good friend." Dad had many friends and little did I know as a twelve-year old that his friends included flag officers, political figures and ordinary people.

I remember Congressman Bob Doughton (November 7, 1863 – October 1, 1954), of Alleghany County, North Carolina, coming to our home in Indian Head, Maryland to visit Dad. Congressman Doughton was a close friend of my grandfather and Dad.

Dad took my brother Bob and I to the Congressional baseball game at Griffith Stadium in Washington, DC in 1953. Some old man sitting next to Dad, kept helping himself to Dad's popcorn. When I asked Dad, why doesn't that old man get his own popcorn, Dad said "Be quiet, that's Sam Rayburn, Speaker of the House."

Walter Wilt, Joe Killen and Kenneth Raby, lifelong friends celebrate Dad's 74th birthday March 1, 1989, Newport News, VA.

Photo by Bill Killen

Don't walk in front of me, I may not follow.
Don't walk behind me, I may not lead.
Just walk beside me and be my friend.

"Give thanks to the Lord, call on His name." –Psalm 105:1

When God Created Mothers
By Erma Louise Bombeck, May 12, 1974

When the good Lord was creating mothers, He was into His sixth day of "overtime" when the angel appeared and said, "You're doing a lot of fiddling around this one."

And the Lord said, "Have you read the specs on this order? She has to be completely washable, but not plastic; Have 180 moveable parts... all replaceable; Run on black coffee and leftovers; Have a lap that disappears when she stands up; A kiss that can cure anything from a broken leg to a disappointed love affair; And six pairs of hands."

The angel shook her head slowly and said, "Six pairs of hands... no way."

"It's not the hands that are causing me problems," said the Lord. "It's the three pairs of eyes that mothers have to have."

"That's on the standard model?" asked the angel.

The Lord nodded. "One pair that sees through closed doors when she asks, "What are you kids doing in there?" when she already knows. Another here in the back of her head that sees what she shouldn't but what she has to know, and of course the ones here in front that can look at a child when he goofs up and say, "I understand and I Love You" without so much as uttering a word."

"Lord", said the angel, touching His sleeve gently, "Come to bed. Tomorrow..."

"I can't," said the Lord, "I'm so close to creating something so close to myself. Already I have one who heals herself when she is sick... can feed a family of six on one pound of hamburger... and can get a nine-year-old to stand under a shower."

The angel circled the model of a mother very slowly. "It's too soft," she sighed.

"But tough!" said the Lord excitedly. "You cannot imagine what this mother can do or endure."

"Can it think?" "Not only think, but it can reason and compromise," said the Creator.

Finally, the angel bent over and ran her finger across the cheek. "There's a leak," she pronounced. "I told You. You were trying to put too much into this model."

"Give thanks to the Lord, call on His name." –Psalm 105:1

"It's not a leak," said the Lord, "it's a tear."

"What's it for?"

"It's for joy, sadness, disappointment, pain, loneliness and pride."

"You are a genius," said the angel.

The Lord looked somber. "I didn't put it there."

I gave Mom a framed copy of Erma Louise Bombeck's "When God Created Mothers" for Mother's Day in the early 1980's. She kept it for years and I thought it would be appropriate to include it in this book as a tribute to Mothers.

Zona Gail Barker Killen (1920-2003)

A few weeks after my mother passed away, my Aunt Grace McMillan sent me a note asking, "wondering how you are" and telling me how she missed the Saturday morning phone conversations with Mom. She included this poem that was read at her mother-in-law's funeral, saying "it sounds so much like Gail." Mom was a "watcher" when I was a teenager and many times was waiting up when I came home. I miss those Saturday mornings phone calls too.

"Give thanks to the Lord, call on His name." –Psalm 105:1

The Watcher

She always leaned to watch for us,
　　Anxious if we were late,
In winter by the window,
　　In summer by the gate;

And though we mocked her tenderly,
　　Who had such foolish care,
The long way home would seem more safe
　　Because she waited there.

Her thoughts were all <u>so full</u> of us,
　　She never could forget!
And so, I think that where she is
　　She must be watching yet.

Waiting till we come home to her
　　Anxious if we are late—
Watching from Heaven's window
　　Leaning from Heaven's gate.

　　　　　　--Margaret Widdemer (1884-1978)

Hey Ma!

Hey Ma! is a familiar sound,
Wherever kids and parents are found.

Teens and tots, and fathers too,
Usually yell for Ma when something is askew.

Either it's Davey wanting a shirt,
Or Carole can't find her skirt.

Pop just out of the tub, lets out a howl,
Hey Ma, where is the towel?

Don Jr., just home from work slams the door,
And tracks up the newly waxed floor.

Then he yells, Hey Ma, when do we eat?
　　And by this time Ma's draggin her feet.

　　　　　　Bill Killen, September 1958

"Give thanks to the Lord, call on His name." –Psalm 105:1

This is my Mama

She's always been there, to see me through,
    When I was little, she tied my shoes.

She made my dresses with love and care,
    This is my mama, she brushed my hair.

This is my mama.

Took me to church so that I could hear,
    'bout how Jesus loved me "Now don't you fear!"

"He will be with you, your whole life through…
    Put your trust in Him, just like I do."

This is my mama.

When I was older and began to date,
    She'd always stay up, no matter how late.

Glad that I was now home… safe and sound,
    She'd go to bed, as she put her Bible down.

This is my mama.

Then on my wedding day, down the aisle,
    Walking in shimmering satin and lace,

Once again her loving hands had made;
    a beautiful wedding dress for my special day.

This was my mama.

So many years, they have come and gone,
    Things are so different, but still I long,

To have my mama as she used to be,
    Love never changes and I know she still loves me.

Brenda Killen Vaccarelli
1985

"Give thanks to the Lord, call on His name." –Psalm 105:1

Never Forget Your Friends

A newlywed young man was sitting on the porch with his father on a hot, humid day; sipping ice tea with his father.

As he talked about adult life, marriage, responsibilities, and obligations, the father thoughtfully stirred the ice cubes in his glass and cast a clear, sober look on his son.

"Never forget your friends," he advised, "they will become more important as you get older."

Regardless of how much you love your family and the children you happen to have, you will always need friends. Remember to go out with them occasionally, do activities with them, call them ..."

"What strange advice!" Thought the young man. "I just entered the married world, I am an adult and surely my wife and the family that we will start will be everything I need to make sense of my life."

Yet he obeyed his father; kept in touch with his friends and annually increased their number. Over the years, he became aware that his father knew what he was talking about.

In as much as time and nature carry out their designs and mysteries on a man, friends were the bulwarks of his life.

After 60 years of life, here is what he learned: Time passes, Life goes on; The distance separates.

Children grow up; children cease to be children and become independent.

And to the parents, it breaks their heart but the children are separated of the parents.

Jobs come and go; Illusions, desires, attraction, sex ... weaken.

People do not do what they should do.

The heart breaks. The parents die.

Colleagues forget the favors. The races are over.

But, true friends are always there, no matter how long or how many miles away they are.

"Give thanks to the Lord, call on His name." —Psalm 105:1

A friend is never more distant than the reach of a need, intervening in your favor, waiting for you with open arms or blessing your life.

When we started this adventure called LIFE, we did not know of the incredible joys or sorrows that were ahead. We did not know how much we would need from each other

Love your parents, take care of your children, but keep a group of good friends. Dialogue with them but do not impose your criteria.

Email from Betty Killen Murphy
June 21, 2017

Read this very slowly…it is profound

Too many people put off something that brings them joy just because they haven't thought about it, don't have it on their schedule, didn't know it was coming or are too rigid to depart from their routine.

I got to thinking one day about all those people on the Titanic who passed up dessert at dinner that fateful night in an effort to cut back. From then on, I've tried to be a little more flexible.

How many women out there will eat at home because their husbands didn't suggest going out to dinner until after something had been thawed? Does the word 'refrigeration' mean nothing to you?

How often have your kids dropped in to talk and sat in silence while you watched 'Jeopardy' on television?

I cannot count the times I called my sister and said, "How about going to lunch in a half hour?" She would stammer, "I can't. I have clothes on the line. My hair is dirty. I wish I had known yesterday, I had a late breakfast, it looks like rain." And my personal favorite: "It's Monday. She died a few years ago. We never did have lunch together.

Because Americans cram so much into their lives, we tend to schedule our headaches. We live on a sparse diet of promises we make to ourselves when all the conditions are perfect!

We'll go back and visit the grandparents when we get Steve toilet-trained. We'll entertain when we replace the living-room carpet. We'll go on a second honeymoon when we get two more kids out of college.

Life has a way of accelerating as we get older. The days get shorter and the list of promises to ourselves gets longer. One morning, we awaken and all we have

"Give thanks to the Lord, call on His name." –Psalm 105:1

to show for our lives is a litany of "I'm going to," "I plan on," and "Someday", when things are settled down a bit."

When anyone calls my 'seize the moment' friend, she is open to adventure and available for trips. She keeps an open mind on new ideas. Her enthusiasm for life is contagious. You talk with her for five minutes and you're ready to trade your bad feet for a pair of Rollerblades and skip an elevator for a bungee cord.

My lips have not touched ice cream in 10 years. I love ice cream. It's just that I might as well apply it directly to my stomach with a spatula and eliminate the digestive process. The other day, I stopped the car and bought a triple-decker. If my car had hit an iceberg on the way home, I would have died happy.

Now go on and have a nice day. Do something you WANT to do, not something on your SHOULD DO list. If you were going to die soon and had only one phone call you could make, who would you call and what would you say?

And why are you waiting?

Make sure you read this to the end; you will understand why I sent this to you.

Have you ever watched kids playing on a merry-go-round or listened to the rain lapping on the ground? Ever followed a butterfly's erratic flight or gazed at the sun into the fading night?

Do you run through each day on the fly? When you ask, "How are you?" Do you hear the reply? When the day is done, do you lie in your bed with the next hundred chores running through your head?

Ever told your child, "We'll do it tomorrow." And in your haste, not see his sorrow? Ever lost touch? Let a good friendship die? Just call to say "Hi?"

When you worry and hurry through your day, it is like an unopened gift thrown away... Life is not a race. Take it slower. Hear the music before the song is over.

Show your friends how much you care. Send this to everyone you consider a FRIEND including me if you consider me a friend. If it comes back to you, then you'll know you have a circle of friends.

To those I have sent this to... I cherish our friendship and appreciate all you do. We have some history together. "Life may not be the party we hoped for but while we are here, we might as well go flying! God bless you and keep you healthy and safe.

Email from Charles Shupienus
May, 2017

"Give thanks to the Lord, call on His name." –Psalm 105:1

Thanksgiving

Pies of pumpkin, apples, mince,
Jams and jellies, peaches, quince
Purple grapes, and apples red
Cakes and nuts and gingerbread
Turkey, Oh a great big fellow
Fruits all ripe and rich and mellow
Everything that's nice to eat
More than I can now repeat
Lots and lots of jolly fun
Games to play and races run
All is happy as can be
For this happiness, you can see
We must thank the One who gave
All the good things that we have
That is why we keep the day
Set aside our mamas say
For Thanksgiving

As recited by Joe W. Killen
Thanksgiving 1983

Joy of Family

Turkey gizzards, jams and nuts
Stuffing, greens and pork butts
Cakes and pastries oh so sweet
Sodium retention, swollen feet
Bubbly cheer with memories made
The joy of family will never fade.

Mark Killen
Thanksgiving 2008

"Give thanks to the Lord, call on His name." –Psalm 105:1

Walter L. Wilt (1920-2008)

INDIAN HEAD, MD — Walter Leo Wilt, 88, died at his home in Indian Head on Thursday, Dec. 18, 2008, after a long battle with cancer.

He was born March 30, 1920, in Westernport, to the late Delbert Wilt and Bertha (Lee) Wilt. He graduated from Fort Hill High School in 1938. In 1941, he joined the Maryland State Police. From May 1944 through June 1946, he served in the United States Marine Corps, returning to the Maryland State Police after an honorable discharge.

He attained the rank of Sergeant with the Maryland State Police and built a reputation of distinction until his retirement from the Waldorf Barrack on Dec. 31, 1971. Prior to his passing, he was the oldest living Maryland State Police retiree.

Funeral Card of Walter Wilt

I knew Trooper Walter Wilt from the time I was six years old. He was a dear friend of my father and a mentor to me and many of my high school classmates. I can never recall seeing him without a smile on his face, even when he had to issue a ticket for speeding or running a stop sign or dealing with misbehaving teenagers.

After I moved to Florida to work in the Space Program he often wrote me and many times his letters included something he had penned. I am honored to include some of his writings in this book. His wife Ruthie was always present in church and it wasn't until later in life that Walter made a profession of faith in Christ. He was baptized and became a member of the Potomac Heights Baptist Church in 2005.

"Give thanks to the Lord, call on His name." –Psalm 105:1

To: APOLLO XI

The Little Stone

Now you've trod
Where only God
has placed a foot before;
You've walked upon the Moon
where ONLY HE has been before.
And yet; your steps though
great they were, they are so
small upon the sea
of space where mightier steps
await to be; and will be
made upon the marks that you,
and others too,
have left upon this broad
infinite sea.

This Moon; our neighbor bright;
this friendly light
is but a speck of sand upon our beach.
It once loomed large in sight,
and dreams and hope, it looms now
larger still; for now we know it's there
to step upon,
and step off from-
To other grains of sand, that
will in some far distant day
withstand the tread of man!

Walter L. Wilt
1969

"Give thanks to the Lord, call on His name." –Psalm 105:1

Brothers of the Badge
Barrack "H" Reunion

Good Humor – Rampant – Good will extant;
Prevailed throughout the eve,
As they mingled there in the warm night air
Camaraderie you could perceive.

Tales were told of action bold,
Not a one doubting the others,
They knew for true, they'd been there too,
And they'd learned to believe their brothers.

Again, they'd met for the 18th time,
And most had long since retired,
But in their pack they all harked back
Through the years when they were hired.

"Once a Marine – Always A Marine"
Is a theme of the U.S.M.C.
The same applies to all the guys
Who careered in the great M. S. P.

"ONCE A TROOPER – ALWAYS A TROOPER",
Are true oft spoken words,
So, they hung in tight in the pale moonlight
Just waiting for their word to be heard.

May God bless these "Brothers of the Badge"
And let them meet in coming years;
For those HE took to their great reward
Will be a subject for Tears!

Present at this vigil – until the hour of eleven
Are named below – known as the "Final Seven".
"Both" (Perkins) – Lester Wilson – "Mike "(Evans) –
"Ted" (Evans) – "Ray" (Presley) – "Billie-T" (Turnball) – and "Louie P" (Pfelts)

Author Ray Presley – Maryland State Police 1965-1995
& Walter L. Wilt - Maryland State Police 1941-1971

"Give thanks to the Lord, call on His name." –Psalm 105:1

Stand with Us.....

Who but I mourn
at the passing of my "brothers",
my comrades in arms
gone now to a glory unknown here –
on earth –
passing on past the throngs of
watchers –
the audience –
the public –
> are they, too, mourners;
> or do they in ignorance stand –
> aware that death passes
> in review........
> but unfeeling that life was in
> such finality spent in their behalf;

>> The lives of my two brother-comrades
>> who walked and worked behind a
>> Badge of Gold
>> for Society's sake and for
>> it a semblance of sanity sustaining,
>> and yet.....
>> and yet to lose –
>> LOSE ALL in an insane,
>> impulsive, frightening moment of
>> fire by an almost insignificant
>> child – who yesterday could have been,
>> and tomorrow again might be
>> amidst that same unknowing throng....

>>> Strangers they were to me,
>>> but brother-comrades still,
>>> for in essence we have
>>> walked shoulder to shoulder through
>>> the festering sores of society for
>>> society's sake and in return
>>> felt society's thanks – and scorn.

>>> SOCIETY – you mourn with us when
>>>> We fall.....
>>> Society – won't you walk with us when
>>>> We stand tall.....?

Walter L. Wilt, 1978

"Give thanks to the Lord, call on His name." –Psalm 105:1

Dad's instructions from 1982

"Hail, King of the Jews"

Hail, King of the Jews, the crowd yelled as they passed,

Hail, King of the Jews, nailed high upon the center mast.

Hail, King of the Jews, save yourself if you think you can,

Hail, King of the Jews, He died for the sins of every man.

Hail, King of the Jews, the jeering crowds screamed and cried,

Hail, King of the Jews, for you and me, He bled and died.

Hail, King of the Jews, He rose from within the grave,

Hail, King of the Jews, have Faith in Christ for He can save.

Hail, King of the Jews, Praise and honor Him all the way,

Hail, King of the Jews, for this is His resurrection day.

Bill Killen, 4 April 1958

"Give thanks to the Lord, call on His name." –Psalm 105:1

The Locker Room

The tile walls were almost obscured by the steam from the showers. The pelting sting of water, relaxing hot water felt great! I could have stayed there all night and enjoyed the relaxing sensation of tiny jet sprays massaging my aching muscles.

The noise of my teammates had finally died down from a dull roar to a murmur and then, all of a sudden, I noticed how quiet it was. Just the sounds of the shower raining its liquid warmth on me and the gurgling of the drain. Finally, I turned off the water and reached for my towel.

Cold! Man was it cold. I rapidly dried my shivering body and headed for my locker, stumbling over tennis shoes, shorts, jockstraps and knee pads. It was cold that night, but then it seemed to me that it was always cold in February.

Slipping into my jockey shorts and reaching for the Mennen "instant bath", I chuckled out loud. Instant bath" – Ray Martin really tickled me, he never takes a shower after practice or after a game. Just "psst-psst" with a squirt to the left and a squirt to the right and he "smells good". At least that's what he thought.

"Smelled" as if he……. well, come to think of it he "smelled" just like this locker room, that's it! Ray smelled like this locker room. Here, smell for yourself. Sweat soaked tennis shoes, with soggy sweat socks that have been left stagnating on top of the lockers for a week, coupled with practice jerseys soaked in "pounds" of sweat, blood and tears, alternately laced with Mennen "Instant Bath" treatments.

After five days of use and then stuffed into a small smelly locker to ferment over the weekend. That smell, that unique odor that haunts gymnasiums and locker rooms with its masculine odor was just how Ray smelled to me.

"Give thanks to the Lord, call on His name." –Psalm 105:1

As I sat down to pull on my socks and shoes, it dawned on me how peaceful the locker room was. Even with the smell of dirty uniforms, the sweet smell of Aqua Velva, Mennen deodorant and Old Spice aroma mixed with the dankness of the locker room, I enjoyed the serenity of the place.

The locker room seemed to have a personality of its own. An athletic personality with a devil may care attitude. Shoes scattered here and there, jockstraps and basketball jerseys draped over locker doors or piled in a heap and ....

" Killen, let's get it moving – I want to go home", yelled the coach.

I rapidly stuffed my shoes, shorts and uniform into my gym bag and grabbed my jacket off the peg. Yep, this place has its own personality, I said to myself as I headed out the door. "Good night Locker Room" I murmured.

"What's that asked the coach?"

"Nothing Coach, just nothing", and I chuckled to myself, "What would he know about a locker room's personality?"

Bill Killen
February, 1958

Parents

They gave us wings and taught us to fly,
    They didn't hold back, the showed us the way.

They gave us the world on a silver tray,
    They taught us of love, and the games people play.

They gave us the strength to stand alone,
    And all the confidence, to make it on our own.

They gave it all, but they'll never know,
    Just how much they taught us to grow.

Jennifer D. Killen
19 February 1986

"Give thanks to the Lord, call on His name." –Psalm 105:1

When the Siren Wails

Early in the morning, or late in the day,
    When the siren wails, men work without pay.
Called from their work, or away from home,
    Volunteers to the rescue, for they've heard the siren blow.

From across the street, or the other side of town,
    They've heard the call for help, a shrill wailing sound.
When they leave the firehouse, hanging on the truck,
    With prayers on their lips, and fingers crossed for luck.

They find the house is burning, as the fire crackles loud,
    While the firemen are quickly working, larger grows the crowd.
The smoke getting thicker and the flames rise up higher,
    And this burning building becomes a dangerous raging fire.

Many firemen arrive and work hard at laying hose,
    while the fire grows redder, like a flaming rose.
Firemen don their masks, and other protective gear,
    Into the burning building, displaying little fear.

Firemen spraying water on the burning blaze,
    while onlookers gossip and others offer praise.
The fire is conquered, yet the smoke lingers still,
    the sightseers have left the scene, they've had their fill.

The firemen take up their hose, and roll it up so neat,
    Most of the men are tired, almost out on their feet.
Back to their firehouse, preparing for another run.
    A fireman's work isn't easy, for its rarely ever done.

The trucks are back in service, the tanks are full again,
    Ready for the next call, no matter where or when.
So, let the whistle blow, and let the sirens wail,
    The Volunteers are always ready, for rarely do they fail.

Bill Killen
11 April 1958

"Give thanks to the Lord, call on His name." –Psalm 105:1

Having grown up a Washington Redskins football fan it was inevitable that I would encounter friends who were die hard Dallas Cowboy fans and Tom Cusick to this day is a Cowboy fan. The Friday before the big game Tom wore his Cowboy hat to work at the Fire and Rescue Institute and fired up his co-workers (Redskins fans). We were invited to the Cusick's home for the game on October 2, 1978. Tom was still fired up and had his cowbell ready to ring every time the Cowboys scored. Well, after all was said and done, at the end of the day more was done than said, especially by the Redskins who won by a score of 9 to 5. Monday morning when Tom arrived at work the following poem had been posted on the bulletin board and all of our co-workers had signed it.

> The drinks were refreshing, deliciously cool,
>> and the Dallas Cowboys looked like "Aprils Fool".

> The chips were crisp, and the dip was hot,
>> as the scoreboard proved the Cowboys were not.

> The easy chair was comfortable, the fireplace charming,
>> the Cowboys soon learned the Redskins were disarming.

> Their receivers couldn't catch, and Roger couldn't throw,
>> because Pardee's Indians were all set to go.

> Landry's plays and Roger's calls didn't jive,
>> because Redskins gave them points four and five.

> But alas, was too late and the game was over,
>> the Redskins had nine and were rolling in clover.

> The Skins record of five wins and no losses,
>> made Landry's Cowboys look like their hosses.

> So, if you are thinking of moving to our town,
>> remember, become a Redskins fan, not a Dallas Clown.

> Now Dallas is good, but the Reskins are better,
> and to help you remember, for your Cowboy hat, here are two feathers.

> So, let this be a lesson to you, and learn it well,
> HAIL TO THE REDSKINS, who stopped you from ringing your bell.

> Bill Killen
> October 2, 1978

"Give thanks to the Lord, call on His name." –Psalm 105:1

A decade later the Redskins rivalry included another co-worker and dear friend, Earnie Davis, a transplanted Texan and Dallas Cowboy fan.

Friday before the game Earnie arrived at work with a bright Dallas Cowboys tie, that took a lot of nerve in Redskins territory.

The Cowboys arrived in DC amidst a lot of hype and hoopla. When they left town, they were eighteen points shy of beating the Redskins. Yep, you guessed it, another poem.

Hail to the Redskins

Dallas came to see the Stadium Jack built,
    twas a beautiful evening, certainly no mystery

The Cowboys met the Indians, and almost got killed.
    Hail to the Redskins, Hail Victory!

Jerry Jones was in a Skybox, in the stadium up on high,
    his team was on the field, ready to play, not to worry.

Where was Earnie Davis and his colorful Cowboys tie?
    Hail to the Redskins, Hail Victory!

So, the first game is over, we are all back at work,
    there will be a second game, another day, another time.

So, wear your tie before the next game. Let's see if it was a quirk.
    If Dallas wins at home, it's your turn to write a rhyme.

And if the Redskins win in Dallas, we'll know the reason why,
    Because they are the better team which we know is no mystery.

We'll be grateful to Earnie, for wearing the Redskins lucky tie.
    Hail to the Redskins, Hail Victory.

Bill Killen
October 14, 1988

"Give thanks to the Lord, call on His name." –Psalm 105:1

Gobble Treats Up!

Pretzels and chips are really neat,
Lots of candy what a treat!

Cookie, cake, chocolate and tart
Too many sweets are not too smart

My Lion is such a brat,
Fed my candy to a rat

Pickles, garlic and fudge on toast
That's the pig I love the most!

Little girlie stole my cracker,
But I'm too smart just to smack her.

Chocolate bars and candy creams
Make me drool and haunt my dreams

Broccoli and eggplant with peas,
Are really yucky covered in cheese.

Go-Cart along mouth open a crack
A bug flew I – what a snack!

Onions really make me gag
Got to toss them in a bag.

Justin P. Keaney
3rd Grade
Blacksburg Elementary

"Give thanks to the Lord, call on His name." –Psalm 105:1

The sun was getting hotter and everything was dry,
The rolling forests were beautiful, a deep shining green,
Smoke was rising and fleeing animals began to cry,
As squirrels chattered loudly while jays began to scream.

Smoke is getting thicker, as flames are reaching higher,
Once tall pines are now ashes, a flaming cherry red,
The once beautiful forest is now a raging fire,
And in it's dangerous path, many creatures law dead.

The fire had quickly spread, from roots to the crown,
Picking up speed and leaving very little slack,
It's flaming fingers reaching across the ground,
Leaving all behind it, a scorched, burnt black.

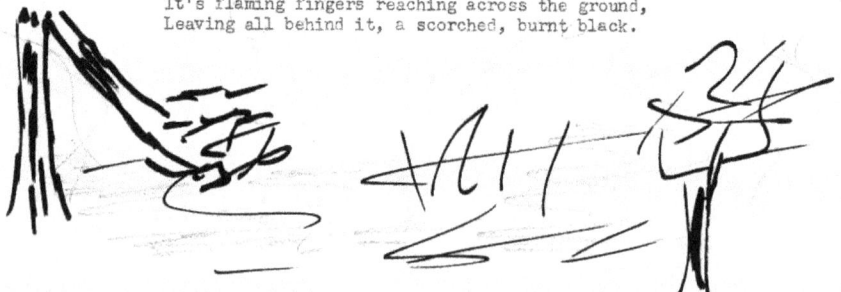

"Ashes" was written in June, 1956 following the "Norman Turkey Farm Fire in St. Mary's County, Maryland. The Norman Turkey Farm Fire was the first major fire response I made after being elected a Junior Member of the Potomac Heights Volunteer Fire Department. The artwork was added sometime in the 1960's.

Bill Killen

"Give thanks to the Lord, call on His name." –Psalm 105:1

A Little Teddy Bear

I'm just a little Teddy Bear, I don't know how to talk,
      I can't hear sounds or words, nor can I even walk.
I have buttons for my eyes, and a little bell in my ear,
      And the fellow who sent me here, thinks you're very dear.

He says he misses you very much, and really loves you so,
      That is why he sent me to you, so I could let you know.
I used to live in an amusement park, so awful far away,
      And I can remember seeing you, with Bill one summer day.

Treat me nice and kind, and I'll learn to love you too,
      And let's hope we'll be happy together, and never blue.
This stuffed Teddy Bear, with my little ribbon of pink,
      Between you and Bill, will be a happy link

By Bill Killen, 6 September 1958

Spring Returns

Swiftly flow the streams,
      Full with winter's melted snows.
Loudly the winds began to scream,
      Cold and stinging as March winds blow.

Fastly March passes us by,
      Winter is over, and Spring draws near.
The cold winds seem to die,
      And again, the happiest season of the year is here.

Robins return, and build their nests,
      Grass starts to grow and flowers bloom.
While other animals wake from their winter's rest,
      Humans seem to have lost their winter gloom.
Spring is so fresh and seems so warm,
      Everyone appears to be happy and gay.
Birds are singing while honey bees swarm,
      Yes, Spring is wonderful, as many say.

Spring comes but once a year,
      And everyone seems to be aglow.
Spring brings freshness and good cheer,
      Yes, Spring has returned, this I know.

By Bill Killen, 3 March 1958

"Give thanks to the Lord, call on His name." –Psalm 105:1

Pocketknife

Knife from my pocket
A tool. A friend. A part of my hand.
Pulled from pocket, and called to flick open
Fingers and palm clench as thumb touches thumbstub.
I wear it well. It's blade well worn.

Its life pointed for purpose.
Out of pocket, then to cut, be cleaned
Be sharpened, and be put back in pocket.

Make me the knife in your pocket.
Daily give me the will to courage off the dresser, to
Be put in your pocket. (to be anywhere else is only lost).

Let me rest in your pocket next to you warm, or hold me
in your hand. Complacent never, but joyful always.
My whole life for your work for my pleasure.

Just to be near you, there with you
Just to be yours, just as I have been bought by
Your son's life. For a life with you.

Daily pull me out to speak your word, which power is
Cutting the straps off sinful loads from the sides
From the shoulders of sinners and saints.

Daily clean my heart of all affections not for you.
In your perfect time remove the dirt and grime
(my painful pleasures) I cling to.

To have a clean heart ready to (work is) worship
like a knife is for cutting and pointing
to you as pleasure of pleasures. My soul's satisfier not pacifier.

Daily sharpen my blade after cutting.
Let your honing and sharpening be like floating
on my back in a pool of your steadfast love.

"Give thanks to the Lord, call on His name." –Psalm 105:1

Make me sharp by your word so sweet I've found
To sing and hear, in return your voice.
You are, My fuel my food my family.

I subject my life to freedom
Constrained controlled by purpose
Cut. Clean. Sharpen.
Share. Renew. Prepare.
Your word. My mind. My life.

Tyler Scott

Seasons

Without a tear trees lose everything once a year.
They don't try and grow to the sky.
They were made to live. Their leaves they were made to give.
Slowly browned they are let go and fall to the ground.
Foliage as fertilizer divinely directed by a supervisor.
They know staying alive at times is the definition of trying to thrive.
If the goal to remain erect do not let leaves hold and collect.
As Snow snaps down branches as winter winds blow.
 See keeping familiar comfort like leaves on a tree.
Just might be the weight that subtle like snowflakes in flight.
Lands like One too many good things, the indulgences of our lands.
compressing compounding suffocating constraining strangling.
death is: a snake slithering in to slowly slip lies into the ears of the deaf).
Some call it fasting; I call it long lasting.

Cycles and seasons providing new reasons to see and savor.
The lover and author of fall winter spring and summer.
Drop your leaves your lover your every silent addiction.
Your small beer, coffee, or that one small fear,
Your tv, food, Netflix, child, hobby, car, or house key.
Let your flesh feel dead like the savior on the cross.
Be bare and empty like the saviors tomb his grave.
Be raised up and made alive like the savior forever,
Like trees in the spring sprouting new buds and blooms.

Tyler Scott
2015

"Give thanks to the Lord, call on His name." –Psalm 105:1

Waking up to Church Bells in Salisbury

Without love we are nothing
but clanging church bells
banging to the tune of amazing grace
Not speaking a word of Christ or his cross
just loud bells clanging for all to notice us
Just loud clanging of good works
That distract even detract when
we act Like we are the main act
Without love we are nothing
but empty clanging church bells

Tyler Scott
January, 2015

What's it worth to you?

Hear it in the trees
as it meets us in the breeze.
Hear it touching leaves
the almost calm before an autumn sneeze.
Tickling trees. Taunting them till
weak in the knees.
Kkkkkrrrackkkkk!!!!!
It gave in...
to the tempting the whispering the whistling
of the wind winding all about its bare bark body.
Softly saying "Relax your roots.
Just try it, just one more small time.
You deserve it for all you have
Withstood. You have done good.

It must not have been an oak.
It must have been a pine tree
Always pining for more,
Or
A Poplar Tree looking for ways to fit in.
Call it Judas or Janice Joplin.
Call it a bought off judge.
But whatever you call it, know it won't be able to hear or feel
The wind it fell for.

Tyler Scott
October 4, 2015

"Give thanks to the Lord, call on His name." —Psalm 105:1

The Dance

His friends knew him as fate.
Hers' said her will would always be free.
All of creation seemed enthralled
Everyone in the great hall
Watched as if they were
All that mattered.
Still no one could believe
"do our eyes deceive"
They whispered to themselves
As the groom danced with his bride
As the bride danced with her groom
"he picked her" they tried to comprehend
"she said yes" their minds still trying to bend
Still they danced
The most awesome romance
Before today She was ever reluctant
never wanting to be led.
Still their bodies swayed
with the tension gone and timing
complete at last they moved in sync
She looked at him like
He was everything as he spun her
Around. She no longer looked
Through him with indifference.
His friends insisted he
Holds the world in his hands
All who knew her persisted
"how could she ever be held?"
All of the living stood stiff in
Admiration as his long lived
Patient plan played out
no longer courting his creation,
but finally bound to his bride beloved.

Tyler Scott
January, 2015

"Give thanks to the Lord, call on His name." –Psalm 105:1

Don't Quit

When things go wrong, as they sometimes will,
When the road you are trudging seems all up hill,
When the funds are low and the debts are high,
And you want to smile but have to sigh,
When care is pressing you down a bit,
rest if you must, but don't you quit.

Life is queer with its twists and turns,
As every one of us sometimes learns,
And many a failure turns about,
When he might have won had he stuck it out'
Don't give up tho' the pace seems slow,
You may succeed with another blow.

Often the goal is nearer than
It seems to a faint and faltering man.
Often the struggler has given up
When he might have captured the victor's cup.

And he learned too late, when the night slipped down,
How close he was to the golden crown.
Success is failure turned inside out—
The silver tint of the clouds of doubt,

And you can never tell how close you are,
It may be near when it seems afar;
So, stick to the fight when your hardest hit—
It's when things seem worse that you mustn't quit.

Bill Killen Collection
Author unknown

"Give thanks to the Lord, call on His name." –Psalm 105:1

Ten Commandments of Human Relations

1. Speak to people. There is nothing as nice as a cheerful word or greeting.

2. Smile at people. It takes 72 muscles to frown-only 14 to smile.

3. Call people by name. The sweetest music to anyone's ears is the sound of his own name.

4. Be Friendly and helpful. If you would have friends, be friendly.

5. Be Cordial. Speak and act as if everything you do is a genuine pleasure.

6. Be genuinely interested in people. You can like everybody if you try.

7. Be generous with praise—cautious with criticism.

8. Be considerate of others. It will be appreciated.

9. Be thoughtful of the opinions of others. There are three sides to a controversy—yours, the other fellow's and the right one.

10. Be alert to give service. What counts most in life is what we do for others.

Excerpt from a presentation by Bill Killen
Navy Area Fire Marshal Workshop 1988

"Nothing is a surprise to God; nothing is a setback to His plans; nothing can thwart His purposes; and nothing is beyond His control." - Joni Eareckson Tada

"Our Christian faith is more than individual chapters and verses from the Bible, it is the sum of them". - Anton Wellbrock

"Give thanks to the Lord, call on His name." –Psalm 105:1

James George Edward Dittrich "Fireman 43" joined the Kennedy Space Center Fire Department May 17, 1966.   I had the distinct pleasure of knowing him as a co-worker and friend, a man of many talents and a sense of humor. He died of a massive heart attack in South Carolina, April 27, 1990. Jim wrote the following poems:

The Last Bell

How many men have walked this land--
    Their names we've known so well,

--and many others, too, have lived
    who've passed before the bell.

Although unnamed for heroic deeds
    more times than tongue could tell

Our gallant brothers sought no fame
    --and passed before the bell

They met their fate sometimes in smoke,
    --sometimes in burning hell.

Saved many lives while giving theirs,
    --to pass before the bell.

If you should see your firemen fight,
    a fire, and do it well.

Remember those no longer here,
    --who passed before the bell.

Jim Dittrich, Fireman,
Kennedy Space Center 1975

"Give thanks to the Lord, call on His name." –Psalm 105:1

The Fireman

The situation's dark, it's late at night--
    In bunks, men toss and turn.

And somewhere fire is burning bright—
    'cause humans never learn.

He's jolted from his fitful dreams
    To answer this alarm,

Each nerve with his body screams-
    God save us all from harm.

He runs toward the waiting truck—
    Jumps on, and hollers—"Go!"

"We'll be back soon, if we're in luck".
    (His heart is pumping so!!!)

He checks his fellow firemen,
    As he's putting on his gear.

"Well, here we go—no sleep again",
    It gets worse year by year.

He doesn't have vast stores of wealth—
    He's just a common man—

He may not be in the best of health,
    But he does what he can

To make life safe for you and me
'cause that's what counts, I guess,

If asked again; "What would you be:
A Fireman?" He says, "Yes!!!"

Jim Dittrich, Fireman
Kennedy Space Center 1968

"Give thanks to the Lord, call on His name." –Psalm 105:1

The Fireman

I am not old, Parson, as I appear to be,
Thirty years of fighting fires has kinda wrinkled me.
I was just a lad when this work I did start,
Night and day, cold and heat, are just a part
Of the screaming of the sirens and the clanging of the bells.

It's been a long, long time since I sat in church,
Seven days a week we old fire boys work
I've just been wondering, sir, if the church could use me,
I'm not good for much, kinda broken up, you see
By the screaming of the sirens and the clanging of the bells.

I will have to limp to serve Him by whom I was made,
Truck skidded one night and badly crushed this leg.
T'was a false alarm they found when the other boys got there,
Guess someone played a joke, just wishing to hear
The screaming of the sirens and the clanging of the bells.

This hand won't be of use, to well do I know,
But in spite of the fire I held the child and carried her from the flat.
Now this ugly scar, let's see, I've forgotten how it came.
Scars like that, Parson, are always in the game
Of the Screaming of the sirens and the clanging of the bells.

Now this old hacking couch, don't pay no heed to it,
I've had it ever since the big theater hit,
Fumes aplenty burned our lungs, but folks were still in there,
So we went in and brought them out, Gases? We didn't care
Amid the screaming of the sirens and the clanging of the bells.

Full peace he made and limped away, broken, but not lost,
I saw him in the cruel marks of Cavalry's cruel cross.
God will send his fiery chariot and bring each crippled child
Up to the Father's house far on beyond the skies.
Amid the flashing of His sirens and the Thundering of His bells.

From the Parson's Diary
The Reverend A. C. Lawton, Sr.

"Give thanks to the Lord, call on His name." –Psalm 105:1

He had no home, He owned no Land
He had no Armies at his command

Yet this very Humble Man
Was known and loved throughout the Land

Thousands and thousands were fully fed
With only a few loaves of bread

He healed the sick, and from her bed
He raised a girl up from the Dead

What sort of man can this be
That raised his hands and calmed the Sea

Or touched the blind and made them see
Or made an Evil Spirit flee

He made Kings shiver and shake
Thinking their kingdoms were at stake

Oh, what a terrible grim mistake
These evil men were soon to make

For thirty pieces, His life they would buy
Soon his disciples would deny

Shake their heads and walk on by
Go on soldiers crucify

Too late now they all knew
This Man was the King of the Jew

I'm not Jewish this is true
But Jesus Christ is my King too.

Robert Craig
Orlando, Florida

"Give thanks to the Lord, call on His name." –Psalm 105:1

As we come to the end of this collection of things to ponder, inspirational poems and stories, jokes, and poetry from family and friends I hope that you enjoyed the humor and wisdom herein. If you found a story or poem that was encouraging, or motivational or a joke that made you laugh, feel free to share it with others.

On this last page I would like to leave you with some important words of wisdom.

I quoted my father at the beginning of the *Family and Friends* section; where he said "the only thing more important in life than your family and your health, is having good friends. However, it is my belief that the only thing more important in life than Your **Salvation**, family and health, in that order, is having good friends. There is no better friend than Jesus Christ our Lord and Savior. I love the hymn "What a Friend We have in Jesus" and He is my friend.

Is He your friend too? If not, He could be. He wants to be your friend.

God says our sin has separated us from Him and that makes it difficult to have the Love of God in our lives, it makes it difficult to have Jesus as our friend.

All we need to do is ask forgiveness for our sins (1 John 1:9).

Invite Christ into our life (John 1:12)

Believe that He has come into our life (Hebrews 11:6)

Thank Him for coming into our life (1 Thessalonians 5:18

Read and pray daily that we might know the promises of this new life that is ours by faith In Christ Jesus (Romans 12:1,2).

All it takes to make Jesus your friend is a simple prayer like this:

"*Lord Jesus, forgive my sins, Come into my life. I receive You as my Lord and Savior. Thank you for forgiving my sins and giving me eternal life. Make me the kind of person that is pleasing to the Father.*

Amen."

"Give thanks to the Lord, call on His name." –Psalm 105:1

ABOUT THE EDITOR

The author is a Fire and Emergency Services Consultant and retired Fire Chief with 69+ years' fire risk management and fire and emergency services management experience, 39 years at the Chief Officer level. Past President/ CEO, International Association of Fire Chiefs and Past President/CEO, National Fire Heritage Center.

One of three surviving members of the original Astronaut Rescue Team at the Kennedy Space Center fire department. He authored the "History of the Apollo and Skylab Astronaut Rescue Team." and has been a contributing author to the books "Firefighters", and "Pass it On", and has been published in several national and international fire service publications.

Recipient of the Military Firefighter Heritage Foundations Lifetime Achievement Award in 2017 and inducted in the Department of Defense Fire Service Hall of Fame in 2013. He was inducted in the Navy F&ES Hall of Fame in 2004.

"Give thanks to the Lord, call on His name." –Psalm 105:1